# classic tv

## Fiona Jerome
## and
## Seth Dickson

**Main Street**
A division of Sterling Publishing Co., Inc.
New York

10 9 8 7 6 5 4 3 2 1

**Library of Congress Cataloging-in-Publication Data Available**

Published by Main Street, a division of Sterling Publishing Co., Inc.
387 Park Avenue South, New York, NY 10016

First Published in Great Britain in 2005 by
Think Publishing
The Pall Mall Deposit
124-128 Barlby Road, London W10 6BL
www.think-books.com

Text © Think Publishing and GCAP Media plc 2005
Design and layout © Think Publishing and GCAP Media plc 2005
The moral rights of the author have been asserted.

Written by Fiona Jerome and Seth Dickson
Edited by Carmela Ciuraru
The *Classic TV* team: James Collins, Rica Dearman, Emma Jones,
Matt Packer, Mark Searle and Lou Millward Tait

Distributed in Canada by Sterling Publishing
c/o Canadian Manda Group, 165 Dufferin Street
Toronto, Ontario, Canada M6K 3H6

For information about custom editions, special sales, premium and
corporate purchases, please contact Sterling Special Sales
Department at 800-805-5489 or specialsales@sterlingpub.com.

ISBN-13: 978-1-4027-3672-8
ISBN-10: 1-4027-3672-X

Printed & bound in Singapore by KHL Printing Co.
The publishers and authors have made every effort to ensure the accuracy and currency of
the information in *Classic TV*. Similarly, every effort has been made to contact copyright
holders. We apologize for any unintentional errors or omissions. The publisher and authors
disclaim any liability, loss, injury or damage incurred as a consequence, directly or
indirectly, of the use and application of the contents of this book.
Cover image: Bettmann/CORBIS

Why should people go out and pay to see bad movies when they can stay at home and see bad television for nothing?

Samuel Goldwyn

# THE AUTHORS WOULD LIKE TO THANK:

Our thanks go to our two enquiring researchers:

Martin Hand, who knows an unfeasable amount about sitcoms, and who is prone to dropping things like "Did you know the man who played Coach in *Cheers* invented Columbo's Dog?" idly in conversation. Martin's research work enriched many sections of the book.

Penny Dash, who knows more about *Sex and the City* than Carrie Bradshaw knows about shoes. Penny's a guru when it comes to scandal, rumors and what *Lost* is really about!

# CONTENTS

# Junior showtime

NOWADAYS KIDS CHOOSE FROM 20 CHANNELS, BUT ONCE UPON A TIME A SMALL HORSE PUPPET WAS ALL WE COULD HOPE FOR

Saturday morning TV: If there's one thing that epitomizes the vast cultural gulf between the UK and the US, it's the competing schools of programming that fight over the airwaves every weekend morning. For decades the Yanks had cheap, badly animated wall-to-wall cartoons (often introduced and linked by other cartoon characters, just to make sure no hint of mundane reality penetrated the kids' fried brains). The Brits countered with cheap, under-financed ensemble TV shows featuring Noel Edmonds, Ant and Dec, Chris Tarrant gunking bemused minor pop stars on *TISWAS* ("This Is Saturday, Watch And Smile"), and Sally James coming over all unintentionally sultry.

| | The US schedule | The UK schedule |
|---|---|---|
| **1950s** | *Howdy Doody Time* | "Daddy, what's a television?" |
| **1960s** | *Captain Kangaroo*<br>*The Beatles* cartoon<br>*Secret Squirrel* | Kids' cinema clubs (as there was still no Saturday morning TV) |
| **1970s** | *Super Friends*<br>*Fat Albert and the Cosby Kids*<br>*Josie and the Pussycats* | *Saturday Scene*<br>*Multi-Colored Swap Shop*<br>*The Saturday Banana* |
| **1980s** | *G.I. Joe*<br>*Kids' Super Power Hour with Shazam*<br>*Slimer & the Real Ghostbusters*<br>*Muppet Babies* | *Going Live*<br>*The Saturday Show* |
| **1990s** | *Saved by the Bell*<br>*Teenage Mutant Ninja Turtles*<br>*WWF wrestling* | *SM:tv* (the first ITV show to trounce the BBC in the ratings)<br>*Live and Kicking* (the show that got trounced) |

> **Television is basically teaching whether you want it to or not.**
> *Muppets* creator Jim Henson

*Sesame Street*, first broadcast in 1969 and a fixture on TV schedules ever since, is almost certainly the most widely-syndicated TV show in the world. Dubbed versions of the much-loved original are broadcast in 120 countries, and there are also at least 20 officially licensed versions of the program, fine-tuned to reflect local cultural norms, including one in Afghanistan. In the course of its three-decade-long run, *Sesame Street* has picked up more Emmys than any other TV show.

The series is known for introducing the Muppets, Jim Henson's inspired creation, and has featured several of the best-loved puppets of all time. Characters such as Big Bird, Oscar the Grouch, the Cookie Monster, Elmo, and Bert and Ernie became so popular that they were spun off into a merchandising phenomenon that has underpinned the finances of the show's permanently strapped-for-cash broadcaster, PBS, for years.

*Sesame Street* has long been notable for its stellar list of guest stars—unusual for a show broadcast on a public television station, rather than a giant corporate-conglomerate network. Among those who have appeared on the program are United Nations secretary general Kofi Annan, movie stars Annette Bening, Yul Brynner, Julia Roberts and Robert De Niro, Broadway diva Ethel Merman, and musician Wyclef Jean (rapping about the wonders of fruit and vegetables). And that's not counting the guest slots awarded to former librarian and First Lady Laura Bush (who read a story called *Wubba Wubba Wubba* to Big Bird) and the band the Goo Goo Dolls.

The show has shown some painful segments, too. Among its most memorable moments was the 1982 episode in which Big Bird discovers that his storekeeper friend Mr. Hooper has died (the episode was first broadcast at Thanksgiving, so that parents would be around to discuss the implications of death with their children), and another in which Big Bird is forced to say good-bye to Snuffleupagus, his imaginary friend.

Dastardly and Muttley never won a race, Penelope Pitstop got her own spin-off series . . . but what of the other contestants in *Wacky Races*, mad cartoon version of Formula One?

| Race no. | Car | Drivers |
|---|---|---|
| 00 | The Mean Machine | Dastardly and Muttley |
| 01 | The Bouldermobile | The Slag Brothers, Rock and Gravel |
| 02 | The Creepy Coupe | The Gruesome Twosome, Big and Little Gruesome |
| 03 | Ring-a-Ding Convert-a-Car | Professor Pat Pending |
| 04 | The Crimson Haybailer | The Red Max |
| 05 | The Pink Compact | Penelope Pitstop |
| 06 | The Army Surplus Special | Sergeant Blast and Private Meekly |
| 07 | The Bullet Proof Bomb | The Ant Hill Mob: Clyde, Ding-a-Ling, Zippy, Pockets, Snoozy, Softy, and Yak-Yak |
| 08 | Arkansas Chug-a-Bug | Luke and Blubber Bear |
| 09 | The Turbo Terrific | Peter Perfect |
| 10 | The Buzzwagon | Rufus Ruffcut and Sawtooth |

> **Educational television should be absolutely forbidden. It can only lead to unreasonable disappointment when your child discovers that the letters of the alphabet do not leap up out of books and dance around with royal-blue chickens.**
>
> Humorist Fran Lebowitz on *Sesame Street* and its ilk

Sci-fi puppet show maker Gerry Anderson was married to his wife Sylvia for 15 years, and she is generally remembered as his most significant collaborator. Perhaps more important to Anderson's success, though, were the musical stylings of the maestro's other long-term partner, bespectacled Blackburn genius Barry Gray, who wrote the music for virtually every Anderson show, including *Thunderbirds* and *Fireball XL-5.*

From his earliest work on *The Adventures of Twizzle* to the mature stylings of *Space: 1999*, Gray was relentless in his pursuit of the innovative and the cutting edge. He was one of the first musicians to be seriously interested in electronic music, and designed his own timing devices—which measured not time but film frames, the better to tailor his music to Anderson's footage. The results are all the more amazing when you realize that all Gray's music was recorded in his own eggbox-lined home in London, which was too small to seat a full orchestra. When a really big sound was called for, the musicians would arrive in relays to record their sessions, which Gray would splice together later.

Remember these imperishable hits?

**Stingray** – The first Anderson theme with real muscle—Gray upgraded from *Fireball XL-5*'s 24-piece orchestra to one with 38 members.

**Thunderbirds** – Dun-dunna-da! Possibly the most memorable kids' TV theme ever composed, the Bondesque parping horns really get across the message that this is a show about wonderful inventions and high-tech gizmos. Gray's score remains a favorite with brass bands all over the world.

**Captain Scarlet** – All together now! "Captain Scarlet / He's the one who knows the Mysteron game / And things that they plan / Captain Scarlet / To his Martian foes a dangerous name / A superman."

**Joe 90** – Gray's famous theme gets its "oomph" from Prisoner-style bongos and the distinctive guitar licks of fretboard maestro Vic Flick.

**Space: 1999** – A kettledrum-fuelled frenzy which somehow packs three distinct movements into less than two minutes of screen time: a brass theme, funky electric guitar (Flick again), then sweeping strings to bring the whole mood down. Probably Gray's most majestic work.

# YOU WON'T RECOGNIZE ME, BUT . . .

**The voice artists behind some of TV's best-loved animated stars . . .**

| | |
|---|---|
| Mel Blanc | Bugs Bunny, Porky Pig, The Ant Hill Mob (all seven) |
| Daws Butler | Yogi Bear, Huckleberry Hound |
| Nancy Cartwright | Bart Simpson |
| Dan Castellaneta | Homer Simpson, Earl in *Cow & Chicken* |
| Henry Corden | Fred Flintstone |
| John Erwin | He-Man |
| June Foray | Rocky the Flying Squirrel |
| Tom Kenny | Narrator of *The Powerpuff Girls* ("The city of Townsville!") |
| Paul Lynde | The Hooded Claw in *The Perils of Penelope Pitstop* |
| Jack Mercer | Popeye (a role he continued to play for 45 years) |
| Don Messick | Scooby-Doo, Muttley |
| Mae Questel | Betty Boop, Olive Oyl |
| Paul Winchel | Dick Dastardly (he also voiced Tigger in *Winnie-the-Pooh* and Fleegle in *The Banana Splits*) |

# NAUGHTY NAUGHTY

*Captain Pugwash* isn't the only children's television show to be the subject of a persistent urban legend. (For those who haven't heard, there never were characters named Master Bates, Seaman Staines, or Roger the Cabin Boy.)

*Fingerbobs* (1972)—one of those charmingly memorable no-budget BBC favorites that repeated endlessly for years on *Watch with Mother*—has also spawned alarming rumors. According to legend, presenter Yoffy (bearded baldy Rick Jones, looking like a hippie refugee from an early Glastonbury festival) got so fed up with his fiddly finger puppets that, having completed the last episode of the second season, he ripped the paper characters from his hands live on air and tore them into small pieces in front of millions of traumatized toddlers.

The truth? There was only ever one season, the show was taped, and slow-voiced Jones was probably the calmest, gentlest kids' TV host, ever.

## HOLY CATCHPHRASE, BATMAN!

The *Batman* TV series, which aired from 1966 to 1968, was notorious for the wilfully execrable lines the writers gave poor Adam West and Burt Ward. Probably the most memorable of the show's numerous verbal tics was the excitable Robin's response to any unexpected development: a blurted "Holy (whatever it might be), Batman!" During the show's 58-episode run, the writers fed Ward more than 350 of these zingers. Among the Boy Wonder's most memorable exclamations:

*Holy . . .*

. . . mashed potatoes . . .

. . . bank deposits . . .

. . . underwritten metropolis . . .

. . . Venezuela . . .

. . . armadillos . . .

. . . uncanny photographic mental processes . . .

. . . rising hemlines . . .

. . . tintinnabulation . . .

. . . Robert Louis Stevenson . . .

. . . interplanetary yardstick . . .

. . . knit one, purl two . . .

. . . astringent plumlike fruit . . .

. . . priceless collection of Etruscan snoods . . .

*. . . Batman!*

## BEFORE *THE SIMPSONS*

. . . there was *Wait Till Your Father Gets Home*, Hanna-Barbera's pioneering 1972 cartoon about the yawning generation gap. All-American pop Harry Boyle (voiced by *Happy Days'* Tom Bosley) has three smart-aleck kids: Chet, Alice, and Jamie, who can't accept their dad's lame parenting techniques. Liberated Alice tries to awaken some spark of feminism in Mrs. Boyle, an apple-pie mom, while nine-year-old Jamie is the family capitalist and will do anything for money. Neighbor Ralph, an unreformed McCarthyite, takes the role later filled by the similarly conservative Ned Flanders. And Harry has a dead-end job, just like Homer (he works in the restaurant supply business).

Although we didn't realize it at the time, Japan's domination of animation styles and children's TV series began back in the late 1970s, when American and British networks began airing *Battle of the Planets*, a re-edited and dubbed version of the classic Japanese animated series *Gatchaman*.

In *Gatchaman*, Kouzaburou Nanbu, a scientist, creates his Science Ninja Team Gatchaman, five teenage kung-fu fighters in bird-styled costumes, to combat the galaxy-wide threat of a terrorist group, Galactor.

In the translated version, Team Gatchaman became G-Force (with cerabonically enhanced powers, whatever those are), a group of orphans called Mark, Princess, Tiny, Keyop, and Jason; and the enemy was renamed Spectra, an alien organization intent on invading Earth, led by the evil Zoltar. In addition to featuring the original five characters, the editors cut in sequences featuring 7-Zark-7, a robot based on Center Neptune who commented on their adventures. Sharp-eyed kids may have noticed that the sequences with 7-Zark-7 didn't look anything like the elegant artwork for the rest of the show—and for good reason, as they were added on later. The robot was necessary because the show's Western editors felt it was far too violent, and cut out the climax to most of the stories. Instead 7-Zark-7 would trundle out and say something like, "Thank goodness G-Force managed to blow up the Black Star, and save the planet from invasion, and are back safe and sound." For about 30 seconds it would switch back to the flowing Japanese style of animation while one of G-Force delivered the moral of the story, and then we'd be encouraged to return for yet another sanitized adventure, next week.

> ## Here comes Muffin, Muffin the Mule / Dear old Muffin, playing the fool.
> Theme song to *Muffin the Mule*, the UK's first children's TV show. Muffin, a puppet who clomped about on Annette Mills's piano, can claim to be its very first star

According to *TV Guide*, which polled American viewers for their favorites, the 20 best-loved animated characters on TV are:

1 Bugs Bunny
2 Homer Simpson
3 Rocky and Bullwinkle
4 Beavis and Butt-Head
5 The Grinch
6 Fred Flintstone and Barney Rubble
7 Angelica Pickles
8 Charlie Brown and Snoopy
9 SpongeBob SquarePants
10 Cartman
11 Bart and Lisa Simpson
12 Fat Albert
13 The Powerpuff Girls
14 Daffy Duck
15 Pikachu
16 Gumby
17 Betty Boop
18 Top Cat
19 Mickey Mouse
20 Popeye

**Children from the age of five to ten should watch more television. Television depicts adults as rotten S.O.B.'s, given to fistfights, gunplay, and other mayhem. Kids who believe this about grown-ups aren't likely to argue about bedtime.**

Model dad and satirist P. J. O'Rourke

## LEADER OF THE GANG

*Top Cat*, one of the most fondly remembered kids' TV shows of the 1960s, was essentially an anthropomorphic version of *Sergeant Bilko*, set in a Manhattan dustbin rather than Fort Baxter. The parallels are obvious to anyone who's seen both programs, and Maurice Gosfield, who played Doberman in *The Phil Silvers Show*, even voiced the feline version of the same character in the cartoon.

| | | |
|---|---|---|
| Sergeant Bilko | = | Top Cat |
| Private Doberman | = | Benny the Ball |
| Colonel Hall | = | Officer Dibble |
| Barbella, Fender, | = | Choo Choo, Fancy, |
| Henshaw, Paparelli | | Brains, Spook |

## CARTOON TEEN IDOLS

There is a tradition of recycling adult television shows as children's offerings by creating simpler cartoon versions, or stories featuring baby versions of established characters. But in the 1970s, a trend for turning real people into cartoon versions of themselves really took off. The trend began when *Scooby-Doo*, paralleling live-action shows, began having weekly celebrity guest stars—drawn in black ink and colored in. Favorite celeb guests were from the Harlem Globetrotters (a troupe of African-American basketball stunt entertainers) who by 1970 had an animated show of their own.

The success of bands like the Osmonds and the Jackson Five among prepubescent fans further fuelled the trend. Because the bands were in such high demand for personal appearances, cartoon shows were created to allow them to be on air without it getting in the way of their schedules. (This happened years before with the Beatles, but few bands since had achieved such staggering success with a predominantly junior audience to warrant it.) *The Jackson Five* lasted for three seasons, from 1971 until 1973 (theme tune: "ABC, Easy As 1-2-3") but *The Osmond Brothers* only ran through 1972 (theme tune: "One Bad Apple Don't Spoil the Whole Bunch, Girl"). Despite intense rivalry for pre-teen hearts between the bands, their shows were in fact masterminded by the same producer team, Joy Batchelor and John Halas.

*The Mickey Mouse Club*, which debuted in 1955 on ABC, was one of the most enduring, and possibly the most influential, of all children's TV shows. Airing daily (Monday was "Fun with Music," Tuesday "Guest Star Day," Wednesday "Anything Can Happen," Thursday "Circus Day," and Friday "Talent Round-Up Day"), the original series featured an all-white cast and ran for 360 episodes before Walt Disney cancelled it when ABC insisted on running more ads. The show continued in heavy rotation into the 1970s, and there were revivals in 1977 and 1989.

Over the years, dozens of wholesome moppets passed through the portals of the Club. Most went on to lead ordinary lives as porn models and convicted felons. But others got bitten by the showbiz bug. All together now: "Who's the leader of the club / That's made for you and me? / M-I-C / K-E-Y / M-O-U-S-E!"

**Christina Aguilera (1993–1994)**
The most popular Mouseketeer of her day became a singing megastar renowned for wearing not many clothes and, sometimes, leather chaps.

**Bobby Burgess (1955–1959)**
Was a featured dancer on *The Lawrence Welk Show* for more than two decades.

**Johnny Crawford (1955–1956)**
Briefly made it as a cowboy star, appearing as Mark McCain, *The Rifleman*'s son, in the long-running hit series (1958–1963).

**Angel Flores (1977)**
Died of AIDS in 1995.

**Annette Funicello (1955–1957)**
From the Club's Queen Bee to B-movie queen, Funicello spent much of the 1960s starring in such Grade Z classics as *How to Stuff a Wild Bikini*, then became a spokeswoman for Skippy Peanut Butter. For many years a conservative, anti-gay activist, she is now battling multiple sclerosis.

**Darlene Gillespie (1955)**
Became a nurse. Sentenced to two years in jail on a dozen counts of conspiracy, securities fraud, mail fraud, obstruction of justice and perjury at the end of 1998.

**Don Grady (1957–1958)**
Hit the soaps as Robbie Douglas, one of the eponymous offspring in *My Three Sons* (1960–1972).

Developed a career as a musician, reaching number 132 on the Billboard music chart with "The Children of St. Monica" (1966). Last heard composing incidental music for The Discovery Channel.

**Kelly Parsons (1978–79)**
Went into the beauty queen biz and made the finals of the Miss USA pageant in 1986. Now working as a hairdresser in Los Angeles.

**Paul Petersen (1955)**
Went on to star, at age 12, in the beloved *Donna Reed Show* (1958–1966), after which his career hit the buffers. Spent years with a Hollywood limousine service, then founded A Minor Consideration in 1990—"an outreach organization that oversees the emotional, financial, and legal protection of kids and former kids in show business," which he still runs.

**Mickey Rooney, Jr. (1956)**
Sacked after a nasty altercation with the Disney paint department. Bizarrely, given his famous father's diminutive stature, Mickey Jr. grew to be over six feet tall, an asset in his adult career as a TV evangelist.

**Britney Spears (1994)**
Reinvented herself as the world's sexiest jailbait teen / pop tart.

**Justin Timberlake (1993–1994)**
Enjoyed a highly publicized romance with fellow Mouseketeer Spears, whom he met on the show. Then shaved off his lovely head of hair to become a down and dirty (relatively speaking) urban music artist guesting on Snoop Doggy Dogg hits.

**Doreen Tracy (1955–1959)**
Posed naked and spread-legged, wearing her Mouseketeer ears, in *Gallery Magazine* back in 1979.

**Lisa Whelchel (1977)**
Played snotty, rich boarding-school girl Blair Warner in long-running NBC sitcom *The Facts of Life*, then starred in dire comedy western *The Wild Women of Chastity Gulch*. Quit showbiz to become a born-again Christian, and author of Christian-themed books such as *The Busy Mom's Guide to Prayer*.

**All television is children's television.**
Richard P. Adler

# Strange adventures

## BUSHY MUSTACHES, SHORT SHORTS AND FRIENDSHIPS TO DIE FOR

## SAME-SEX SHENANIGANS

A good number of buddy-buddy shows—usually featuring a close, bantering friendship between two hunky male leads—have attracted speculation as to the true nature of the relationship between the characters. Directors and stars can issue denials till they're blue in the face, but they'll never persuade some viewers that Starsky and Hutch weren't doing a lot more than just relieving themselves when they popped to the loo at Huggy Bear's. Among the closet couples that have attracted a lot of speculation are:

### 1. Bodie and Doyle, *The Professionals*
A pair of armed cops who were just too sexy for their shirts.

### 2. Kirk and Spock, *Star Trek*
There must have been some sort of heart beating within that frozen, emotionless exterior. And Spock looked like he might warm up with a few beers inside him, too.

### 3. Batman and Robin, *Batman*
Bruce Wayne and his ward shared a superhero secret . . . but was there more to their partnership than a burning desire to fight crime?

### 4. Hannibal Heyes and Kid Curry, *Alias Smith & Jones*
Long days in the saddle with only your friend and his horse's backside to contemplate can do strange things to a man. Especially when you're starring in a series that involves an awful lot of tying people up.

### 5. *Cagney & Lacey*
Oh, come on . . . the ineffectual Harvey was born to be a beard.

### 6. Basil Fawlty and Manuel, *Fawlty Towers*
The doglike devotion, the passionate rows—some sort of S&M thing going on, we'd guess.

### 7. Carter and Regan, *The Sweeney*
Tough guys share a car, maybe more, in homophobic 1970s London. All that obsessive boasting about "birds" and "shagging" was just a necessary front.

### 8. Bert and Ernie, *Sesame Street*
If you don't want people to talk, don't share the same bedroom for 35 years.

# WE'RE STILL WAITING FOR THE BIONIC FETUS

*Six Million Dollar Man* Steve Austin (Lee Majors) wasn't the only man-machine wandering around the US TV landscape in the late 1970s. The show was so popular that the producers wasted no time in launching a series of cash-ins, sorry, spin-offs and TV movies which clogged the airwaves for the next several years. These saw the introduction not only of other metallically implanted characters, but an increasingly ropey series of excuses to explain why the characters' near-critical injuries always seemed to involve trauma to the legs. That bionic family in full:

| The bionic. . . | Identity | Bionic bits |
| --- | --- | --- |
| Man | Steve Austin, played by Lee Majors | Both legs, right arm, left eye |
| Woman | Jaime Sommers, played by Lindsay Wagner | Both legs, right arm, right ear |
| Boy | Andy Sheffield, played by Vince Van Patten | Legs, again |
| Dog | Max, the million-dollar mutt, played by Bracken | All four legs, jaw |
| Criminal | Barney Miller, the Seven Million Dollar Man, played by Monte Markham | Both legs, both arms |

**The violence, I can't even talk about. We don't do a lot of violent shows. When I started in television, breaking a pencil was a violent act.**

Veteran TV producer Aaron Spelling, the man behind *Charlie's Angels*, *Beverly Hills 90210* and *Hart To Hart*

## "IT'S A TOTALLY NEW CONCEPT, B. D."

It took *Doonesbury* creator Gary Trudeau to truly skewer the pretensions of NBC's *Miami Vice*, which was, in the late 1980s, the hottest show on TV. Don Johnson made millions of women's hearts beat faster, and inspired far too many young men to go out in chilly northern climes wearing shoes without socks and jackets with the sleeves rolled up. When fans weren't getting fashion tips, they were lapping up the exotic locations and sports cars.

In one sequence of the Pulitzer prize-winning comic strip, bikini model Boopsie lands a role in the series and invites live-in boyfriend B. D. to watch a few episodes with her. "OK," she tells him at one point. "Here comes the love interest." Pause. "The love interest's a car?" B. D. asks incredulously. Boopsie frowns: "It's a totally new concept, B. D."

## WORST. UNIFORMS. EVER.

It's been nearly a quarter of a century now since Larry Wilcox and Erik Estrada last cruised the highways of California wearing their Nazi-style gray polyester breeches and their black boots—and they still haven't forgiven one another. The two actors, who played officers Jon Baker and Francis Llewellyn "Ponch" Poncherello on NBC's low-rating but long-running *CHiPs*, never really got along. Maybe it had something to do with all that helmet hair. "The set was divided into two camps," Estrada wrote in his autobiography. "Larry's people and my people. As soon as the director called 'cut,' we'd head off in different directions without saying another word to each other."

By the time the final season of the show was ready to film, Wilcox was about ready to quit. After one argument too many, he left, sending *CHiPs* into a terminal spiral. Estrada's new partner, Tom Reilly, was fired almost as soon as he arrived after yet another falling out, and the show was cancelled shortly thereafter, just as Ponch got his third partner in less than a year.

The original pair got back together for a TV movie in 1999, but nothing much came of it. Wilcox now works in pharmaceuticals, and Estrada has made a TV comeback of sorts, landing a starring role in *Dos Mujeres, Un Camino*, Mexico's top-rated TV drama.

There's never been a show quite like it when it comes to setting tonsorial trends: *Magnum, P.I.*—aka "The Tom Selleck Mustache Show"—encouraged a whole generation of men to think that they, too, could look as good as the craggily handsome TV detective simply by sprouting a bit of facial fungus. It didn't work of course; Selleck's mustache was uniquely gorgeous, thick and heavy, and so very manly. But there was always more to Selleck than just a mustache. Here are eight fast facts about the man behind TV's greatest-ever lip-topper:

1.  Selleck is a close pal of the ailing Charlton Heston, and an active member of the pro-gun National Rifle Association.

2.  He famously lost out on the chance to play Indiana Jones when Steven Spielberg's shooting schedules clashed with the demands of *Magnum*. Second choice Harrison Ford got the role instead.

3.  He started out as a model, getting his acting break on the TV soap *The Young and the Restless* in 1967. His film career never really overcame his debut as the young stud who ogled an aging Mae West in the celebrated stinkeroo *Myra Breckenridge* (1970); his only notable starring role since then was in *Three Men and a Baby* (1988), although he scored a critical hit in a supporting role to Kevin Kline in *In and Out* (1997). His attempted big-screen comeback in *The Love Letter* (1999) went belly up when it was released in the same week as the eagerly anticipated *Star Wars: Episode 1*.

4.  He made one of the most memorable guest appearances on *Friends*, season 2, playing Monica's old flame Dr. Richard Burke (complete with twinkling eyes and trademark 'stache), briefly reappearing in season 3.

5.  A member of California's National Guard, Selleck was mobilized when the Watts riots paralyzed Los Angeles in 1965.

6.  He volunteers at the Los Angeles Mission, which helps the homeless.

7.  US activist group Queer Nation attempted to out Selleck as gay in the early 1990s. He called a press conference to deny the claims.

8.  Selleck became so synonymous with his mustache that when he was desperate to generate publicity for his 1997 movie *In and Out* he shaved half of it off—and was rewarded with a guest slot on NBC's *Late Night with Conan O'Brien*. Since then, he's gone largely hairless. For shame!

The show ran for five seasons, but there were only six Angels. Can you remember who was whom?

| Angel | Played by | She was . . . |
| --- | --- | --- |
| **Sabrina Duncan** | Kate Jackson | The tall sensible one who wore trousers |
| **Kelly Garrett** | Jaclyn Smith | The brunette one |
| **Jill Munroe** | Farrah Fawcett | The one with the biggest hair and most protuberant nipples |
| **Kris Munroe** | Cheryl Ladd | Jill's sister, drafted in when Fawcett quit after the first season |
| **Julie Rogers** | Tanya Roberts | The redheaded one |
| **Tiffany Welles** | Shelley Hack | The one from the last couple of seasons you can never quite place |

## DA PLANE! DA PLANE!

Herve Villechaize may have stood only 3 ft 11 in, but the *Fantasy Island* star—he played Tattoo in the hit show—soared to truly heroic stature in his sleazed-up private life. Prior to committing suicide in 1993, at the age of 51, Villechaize enjoyed playing "Spin the Midget" with his female acquaintances; whoever won the spin got a dinner date and—according to a coy profile on *E!*, the entertainment channel—whatever else would transpire. In his latter years, Villechaize took to chugging down beers while watching reruns of his only real starring role, all the while slurring insults at producer Aaron Spelling, whom he insisted had underpaid and failed to appreciate him. By the end he was downing two bottles of wine a night (a good deal for a man who weighed only 90lb), had blown his $3.6 million fortune, and was earning only $500 a week. Tormented by constant pain from internal organs that were simply too big for his body, Villechaize pressed a cushion against his heart in his California home, and shot himself once in the chest.

> Part of the success of *Magnum, P.I.* stemmed from the combination of familiar hard-boiled action and exotic locale. Just as important perhaps, the series was one of the first to regularly explore the impact of the Vietnam War on the American cultural psyche. Many of the most memorable episodes dealt with contemporary incidents triggered by memories and relationships growing out of Magnum's past war experiences. Indeed, the private investigator's abhorrence of discipline and cynical attitude toward authority seem to stem from the general mistrust of government and military bureaucracies that came to permeate American society in the early 1970s.
>
> Rodney Buxton, The Museum of Broadcast Communication, on the importance of *Magnum, P.I.*

## MY OTHER CAR'S A VOLVO

The Saint's iconic Volvo P1800 (trust us: it looked cooler than you'd think) was one of the best-loved features of the 1960s TV series, but things were very nearly very different. Leslie Charteris, the author who created the suave gentleman thief Simon Templar, had equipped his hero with a mythical beast of a car called a Hirondel in the original books. When it came time to put his work on screen, the producers asked Jaguar to supply them with the closest equivalent available in 1962, a sporty new E-type. Jaguar, according to legend, were happy to oblige, but this was the early 1960s, unions still ruled the roost in the automotive industry, and the company could not make good on its promise to deliver in time for filming to begin. As the first day of principal photography loomed, the series' star—a pre-Bond Roger Moore—offered to lend the producers his own car to help out. And that's why Templar drove a Volvo coupe throughout the show's seven-year run.

*The Saint* saved the P1800 in the UK. Volvo had been about to discontinue production of its right-hand drive version, but the series prompted such demand for the car that it continued to be made for several more years.

It's a matter of record that when the British channel ITV went into production with *The Return of the Saint* (1979), Jaguar was swift to make amends for past mistakes, promptly supplying Ian Ogilvy with a new white XJS.

In most countries David Hasselhoff, the perma-tanned star of *Knight Rider* and *Baywatch*, is considered a bit of a joke. But in Germany he's a legend—a rock god whose song *Looking for Freedom* (a cover of an old German favorite, *Auf Der Strasse Nach Suden*) was not only number one for 12 straight weeks in 1989, but was directly credited (not least by Hasselhoff himself) with bringing down the Berlin Wall.

Hunky Hoff's career as an international force for good got underway when his song—"I've been looking for freedom / I've been looking so long / I've been looking for freedom / Still the search goes on" soared up the charts just before the collapse of Communism in East Germany. The rousing soft rock anthem was adopted by protesters and may even have been sung by some of those wielding sledgehammers and pickaxes when the wall came down in November. What certainly is true is that the Hoff went on to perform his hit—clad in a pair of illuminated leather trousers and perched on the remains of the wall itself—to a live audience estimated at more than a million that New Year's Eve.

The story might have ended there but for an interview the warbling actor gave to a German film magazine in 2004, in which he complained bitterly that his pivotal role in the reunification of a great country was being written out of history. "I find it a bit sad that there is no picture of me hanging on the walls of the Berlin Museum at Checkpoint Charlie," he announced, without irony, to what became worldwide derision.

## I think *Baywatch* is such a hit because of the weather.

Pneumatic *Baywatch* actress Gena Lee Nolin gives her considered opinion on the series' immense popularity

Since first hitting the small screen back in 1953, TV's best-loved outlaw has been played by some of the finest thespians in the business . . . and Jason Connery.

### Patrick Troughton
**Robin Hood, 1st season, 1953**
Yes, that is Dr. Who poncing around in the wrinkly breeches.

### Richard Greene
**The Adventures of Robin Hood, 1953**
The fondly remembered British TV series featured Donald Pleasance as Prince John and a very young Paul Eddington as Will Scarlet.

### David Watson
**The Legend of Robin Hood, 1968**

### Len Carlson / Ed McNamara
**Rocket Robin Hood, 1968**
Robin and friends take to the spaceways in this fondly remembered if crappily animated Canadian series from Ralph Bakshi, who went on to make a cartoon version of *The Lord of the Rings*. The Merry Men live on Sherwood Asteroid and are armed with "deadly" electro-quarterstaffs. So that's where George Lucas got the idea for light sabers from.

### Martin Potter
**The Legend of Robin Hood, 1975**

### Richard Gautier
**When Things Were Rotten, 1975**
Short-lived Mel Brooks TV outing that presaged the much-derided *Robin Hood: Men in Tights*. For once it seems Brooks's wit deserted him when it came to judging Charles Strouse's title song:
> "Once upon a time when things were rotten
> Not just food, but also kings were rotten
> Everybody kicked the peasants
> Things were bad and that ain't good
> Then came Robin Hood."

### Michael Praed / Jason Connery
**Robin of Sherwood, 1984**
The Saxon Robin gets an Aryan makeover when Connery joins the cast.

### Wayne Morris
**Maid Marian and Her Merry Men, 1989**
Tony Robinson's feminist spin on the legend reduces Robin to the role of an incompetent tailor and features Red Dwarf's Danny John-Jules as one of the Merry Men.

**Thor Bishopric**
*Young Robin Hood*, 1992

**Matthew Porretta / John Bradley**
*New Adventures of Robin Hood*, 1997
Another cruddy animation, French
this time, dubbed for the US market.

**Samuel Ball**
*Captain Jackson*, 1999
A Sherwoodian nadir. Robin "stars"
alongside Toothy Trotters and Dr.
Screwloose in this mindless cartoon.

**Christopher B. McCabe**
*Back To Sherwood*, 1999

## HEROES IN SPANDEX

Comic books have always been a rich source of inspiration for TV producers looking for something fast paced and capable of entertaining children of all ages. From the 1950s (almost as soon as they could work out how to get someone to lie on a block of glass, arms out, and film it to look like he's flying) Superman was a solid favorite. Recently he's been dusted off as a teen hero in WB Television Network's *Smallville*, dealing with evildoers and raging hormones simultaneously, while 1993's *Lois and Clark* focused on the grown-up hero's romantic life.

Batman only had one live action outing, a campy 1960s offering with a host of guest stars and gimmicks, but numerous cartoon versions have been made alongside the successful film franchise. The 1970s saw the shapely Lynda Carter taking the role of Wonder Woman, the Amazon fighter with a lasso of truth and magic bracelets. And Marvel Comics' quintessential angst-ridden teen hero, Spider-Man, got his first live action show in 1977. But the most popular comic book hero of the 1970s was undoubtedly the Incredible Hulk. Although they look crude now, Bill Bixby's transformation into Lou Ferrigno—a body builder in a wild wig daubed with green paint—were tremendous when you were in kindergarten.

It takes a big film budget to bring characters like the X-Men and Fantastic Four alive—TV budgets can just about stretch to one costumed hero, but the cost of effects for half a dozen, often at the same time, are apparently prohibitive.

# Side
# splitters

FROM SLAPSTICK TO SATIRE, THE BEST
SITCOMS FROM BOTH SIDES OF THE POND

Running from 1974–1985, *Happy Days* was an immensely popular and highly idealized look at life in the late 1950s, inspired by the success of the George Lucas film *American Graffiti*.

The show rapidly turned into a franchise, with several spin-offs. The first was *Laverne and Shirley*, with Cindy Williams and Penny Marshall, still set in the 1950s, but moving the excitable girls to Los Angeles. It was a huge success and prompted a further spin-off in 1977, *Blansky's Beauties*, produced by the same team as *Happy Days*. Dad Howard Cunningham's cousin, Nancy Blansky, is chaperone to a gaggle of vacuous Vegas showgirls and the innocent young men they attract (including *Happy Days'* Scott Baio). Despite staring Nancy Walker (Ida Morgenstern from *Rhoda*) the series was short-lived. Even so, in 1982, they tried again with *Joanie Loves Chachi*, which followed the teenage lovers as they moved to Chicago and Chachi tried to start a singing career.

But the strangest and most successful spin-off was 1978's *Mork and Mindy*, about a single woman (played by actress Pam Dawber) who befriends an alien, played by Robin Williams. Mork was a character in a dream-sequence episode of *Happy Days*. In turn *Mork and Mindy* spun-off *Out of the Blue*, a series about an angel living with a 1970s family (both of which, god help us, probably led to the creation of *ALF*). *Mork and Mindy* also became a successful animated show, along with *Fonz and the Happy Days Gang*, and *Laverne & Shirley*.

The final legacy of *Happy Days* was among TV critics. As the series progressed, plots became increasingly stranger, until one episode revolved around the Fonz doing a water-ski jump over a shark. Critics declared this was a sign the show was definitely past its best, and took to using the phrase "jumping the shark" to refer to the point at which other series passed their sell-by date.

> The remarkable thing about television is that it permits several million people to laugh at the same joke and still feel lonely.
>
> T. S. Eliot

Set in the dingy garage of the Sunshine Cab Co. in New York City, *Taxi* brought together a talented cast playing a bunch of ordinary joes, most of whom have wound up driving a cab for the wrong reasons, under the control of their tyrannical boss, Louie, played by Danny DeVito. The script constantly plays with the notion that Louie isn't as mean-spirited as he seems, but he invariably manages to come out a complete heel. The show ran for six years and won 18 Emmys and 4 Golden Globes.

*Taxi* confronted many issues comedies didn't usually tackle in 1978, such as bisexuality, drug addiction, and street kids, and featured a zany mix of characters. Alex Reiger (Judd Hirsch) was the decent Everyman figure, Marilu Henner the forced-to-be-tough female driver, and Christopher Lloyd a preacher who may or may not have been completely barking. But the show was stolen by Andy Kaufman playing Latka Gravas, the sympathetic immigrant mechanic who suffered from multiple personality disorder. Latka represents everyone who's ever

been bewildered by a new experience. Kaufman wasn't keen to make a sitcom, but was persuaded by the multiple personality disorder, which gave him carte blanche to show off his talents, including one episode where he became just like Alex.

Kaufman had come to prominence on *Saturday Night Live*, but was famously banned from the show by a public vote after performing his well-known female wrestling sketch. His comedy had always been character-based and mind-bending, beginning with stand up featuring "Foreign Man," an excruciatingly bad impressionist from the fictional island of Caspiar. On *Letterman Show* appearances, he would talk about children he didn't have, while promoting a feud with a wrestler, which also turned out to be bogus. He created a cantankerous lounge singer who opened his shows and for many years was believed to be a separate person. When he died in 1984, at age 35, of lung cancer, many people believed this was just another of his hoaxes and rumors persist that he had plastic surgery and is actually Jim Carrey.

## TOP 10 BEST BRITISH CATCHPHRASES

1. **"Just like that"** – Tommy Cooper, who starred in many shows, including *Cooper, Just Like That*
2. **"I didn't get where I am today without . . ."** – C. J. Reginald Perrin, *The Fall and Rise of Reginald Perrin*
3. **"You plonker, Rodney!"** – Del Boy, *Only Fools and Horses*
4. **"Yeah, but no, but yeah, but"** – Vicky Pollard, *Little Britain*
5. **"Stupid boy"** – Captain Mainwaring, *Dad's Army*
6. **"I'm free!"** – John Inman as Mr. Humphries, *Are You Being Served?*
7. **"I don't believe it!"** – Victor Meldrew, *One Foot in the Grave*
8. **"Garlic bread, I've tasted it, it's the future"** – Peter Kay, *Phoenix Nights*
9. **"I have a cunning plan . . ."** – Baldrick, *Blackadder*
10. **"Suits you, Sir!"** – Paul Whitehouse and Mark Williams as the Gentlemen's Outfitters, *The Fast Show*

## ALTERNATE WORLDS OF COMEDY

When they began making *Only Fools and Horses*, one of the most successful comedies the BBC has produced, Nicholas Lyndhurst was signed up to play Del Boy's feckless younger brother Rodney quickly, as was Lennard Pearce for the role of wily Grandad. But writer John Sullivan and director Ray Butt couldn't find their Del Boy. The first possibility was Scottish actor Enn Reitel, best known as a voice actor for series like *Spitting Image*. Unlike David Jason who eventually got the part, Reitel looked like an older version of Lyndhurst. When Reitel turned it down, they considered noted thespian Jim Broadbent, but he had other commitments. Broadbent went on to make three appearances in the series as DCI Roy "The Slag" Slater, an over-the-top, Sweeney-style copper. Then Roger Lloyd Pack was in the frame, but the long-faced actor so closely resembled the look the creators had envisaged for another character, Trigger, that he was given that role instead.

In the end, after watching a repeat of *Open All Hours*, Sullivan settled on David Jason, but with grave misgivings, because he associated Jason with softer, underdog parts. Ray Butt had more faith. Basing his portrayal of the loveable wide boy on a builder, Derek Hockley, with whom he'd worked as an electrician before taking up acting, David Jason immediately made the role his own.

It doesn't matter what you all think. I know I'm a straight man! I know it!

*[cue music, as song begins ]*

And I'll tell you whyyyyyyy . . .

I love baseball, and boxing,
messing around with tools!
Six-packs, and wrestling,
and smoking a pack of Kools.

I love watching Steve McQueen
movies on the late, late show!
And push-ups, and jumping jacks,
don't you know!

What I really, really love
more than anything . . .
are boobies! Boobies!

Boobies in the morning,
boobies in the spring!
Boobies in my face,
boobies are everything!

Boobiiieeesss!!

I think I just set the record straight, would you say? We've got a great show for you tonight! I'm not gay! Jay-Z's here, with Lenny Kravitz and Beyoncé! So stick around—I'm not gay—we'll be right back! I'm not gay! I'm not . . . gay!"

Eric McCormack hosting *Saturday Night Live*, making light of so many fans assuming he is gay because he plays a gay man in *Will & Grace*

## THE SHOW WITH THREE NAMES

We think of it as *Sgt. Bilko*, and it began life under the title *You'll Never Get Rich*, but actually the show, which revolutionized American sitcoms was called *The Phil Silvers Show*. Hugely influential both in America and in the UK, it starred Phil Silvers as Master Sergeant Ernie Bilko, who, rather than fighting, spent his time in the army running scams (right under the nose of the bemused post commander) while purportedly running a carpool. Although it ran for only five seasons, the show was rerun many times in the early days of television, until the advent of color made it look old-fashioned.

Younger audiences were introduced to the delights of bullying, charming, manipulative Bilko in the form of *Top Cat* (called *Boss Cat* in the UK for many years because there was already a brand of cat food called Top Cat). Debuting in 1961, it featured a streetwise alley cat (voiced by Arnold Strang) and his gang of none-too-bright hangers on, who nevertheless always got one over on their nemesis, Officer Dibble. In 1963, Silvers returned for *The New Phil Silvers Show*. Instead of Bilko, he played a similar character, Harry Grafton, maintenance supervisor at a large industrial plant, but the series only lasted one season. Bilko's last stand came in 1996, when Steve Martin took on the Bilko role for an (unsuccessful) feature film.

## KEEPIN' IT REAL

**Over the years a stellar range of musical stars have agreed to voice their cartoon equivalents for *The Simpsons*, even though their portrayal may have been less than flattering:**

50 Cent ● Aerosmith ● The B-52's ● Tony Bennett
Blink-182 ● James Brown ● David Byrne ● Elvis Costello
Cypress Hill ● Mick Jagger ● Elton John ● Tom Jones
Little Richard ● Paul McCartney (with Linda McCartney)
Metallica ● Willie Nelson ● *NSYNC ● Dolly Parton
Radiohead ● R.E.M. ● The Ramones
Red Hot Chili Peppers ● Keith Richards ● Linda Ronstadt
The Smashing Pumpkins ● Sonic Youth
Britney Spears ● Sting ● James Taylor
Justin Timberlake ● U2 ● Barry White ● The Who

Nicolas Colasanto found lasting fame playing Coach on *Cheers*. He was a friend of Peter Falk and much earlier on in his career directed two early episodes of *Columbo*. "'Etude in Black' (1972) deserves a special mention because it marks the debut of the dog, Columbo's pet basset hound," he later reminisced. "Dog had his origins in NBC's persistent demands for another continuing character, Levison and Link merrily decided to comply with the network's wishes.  They talked to Steven Bochco who was writing the opening episode of the second season, who wanted a young cop to be his sidekick. I said let's give him a dog."

Peter Falk wasn't so keen on the idea, as he thought the detective already had too many trademarks, but when he saw the prospective pooch he changed his mind. The animal chosen for the part was a large, ugly bloodhound required to loll around a great deal, and only jump into action at the most inopportune moments. *Columbo* spends 'Etude in Black' trying to figure out a name for his new companion ("This dog needs a name that will give him some stature. He needs all the help he can get") but in the end simply settles on Dog. When the original dog died, a second animal was cast, and viewers never noticed, thanks to skillful application of makeup to make the younger substitute appear older and more worn.

Dog made many memorable appearances, but not in Colasanto's second *Columbo* episode. For that one, he had to be content with Johnny Cash murdering Ida Lupino!

**Don't mention the war! I mentioned it once, but I think I got away with it. All right. So! It's all forgotten now, and let's hear no more about it. All friends now. That's two egg mayonnaise, a prawn Goebbels, a Hermann Goering, and four Colditz salads.**

John Cleese (Basil Fawlty, *Fawlty Towers*) does his bit for European unity, in possibly the series' most famous comedy moment

# "I'M LISTENING"

**During his 12-year stint as Seattle's favorite radio psychiatrist, Dr. Frasier Crane received calls from a plethora of troubled stars, including:**

Gillian Anderson ● Kevin Bacon ● Halle Berry ● Mel Brooks
Cyd Charisse ● Cindy Crawford ● Billy Crystal ● Macaulay Culkin
Phil Donahue ● David Duchovny ● Hilary Duff ● Anthony Edwards
Gloria Estefan ● Carrie Fisher ● Jodie Foster ● Art Garfunkel
Tommy Hilfiger ● Ron Howard ● Eric Idle ● Jay Leno ● Stephen King
Timothy Leary ● Malcolm McDowell ● John McEnroe
Helen Mirren ● Mary Tyler Moore ● Jerry Orbach ● Bonnie Raitt
Christopher Reeve ● Rob Reiner ● Neil Simon ● James Spader
Ben Stiller ● Randy Travis ● Garry Trudeau
Stanley Tucci ● Eddie Van Halen ● John Waters
Rufus Wainwright ● Elijah Wood ● Pia Zadora

## *THE FLYING NUN* – CATHOLIC PROPAGANDA?

*The Flying Nun*, when you summarize it, sounds so odd that people often think you're pulling their leg. Back in the late 1960s, award-winning actress Sally Field plays novice Sister Bertrille, in a series whose storylines revolve around her flying off, usually into the middle of a "hilarious" situation, much to the disapproval of her Mother Superior. The flying was not a side-effect of exposure to gamma rays or some such, but a result of her small stature and heavily starched habit.

You might think the Catholic Church would be up in arms at a series that made fun of nuns and convents, but actually ABC's hit was made with the approval of the Church, then going through a phaze of modernization, and was praised by nuns as being the most accurate portrayal of convent life ever shown on television. The series targeted teenage girls, a key audience for the Church, which was experiencing an alarming decline in girls wanting to take holy orders. However Sally and her stiff wimple didn't seem to do the trick. During the four years the show was broadcast (1967–70) the overall number of nuns fell 10%. Even if it didn't bolster the ecumenical sisterhood, though, the show did its bit to promote anti-counterculture, anti-women's lib sentiments.

When you've revolutionized British comedy, what do you do for the rest of your life? Here are some highlights:

### Graham Chapman:

*Odd Job*, a feature film developed from one episode of *6 Dates with Ronnie Barker*, where he took the lead role after Keith Moon of the Who was unable to play it.

*Out of the Trees*, a sketch show where all the material was based around a discussion between two linguists about the origin of a word.

*Yellowbeard*, a mad pirate comedy also starring Cheech and Chong, Peter Cook, Madeline Kahn, and Marty Feldman.

### John Cleese:

*Fawlty Towers*, possibly the most perfect sitcom ever made.

*A Fish Called Wanda*, very polished and very funny, much better than its follow-up *Fierce Creatures*, which nonetheless raises a giggle.

*Whoops Apocalypse!* the much-underrated comedy written by Andrew Marshall and David Renwick.

### Terry Gilliam:

*Jabberwocky*, a filth-encrusted medieval fantasy that brought together the Pythons with sitcom legends Harry H. Corbett, John Le Mesurier, and Warren Mitchell.

*Brazil*, a visually stunning, but incredibly grim, science-fiction fable,

heavily influenced by George Orwell.

*12 Monkeys*, Gilliam's big Hollywood hit, in which Bruce Willis is sent to warn us about how horrid the future will be.

### Eric Idle:

*Rutland Weekend Television*, in which a small ensemble cast spoofed the low-budget output of a regional TV station.

*The Mikado*, a TV production directed by John Michael Phillips, where he was a revelation as Ko-Ko.

*Spamalot*, his comedy smash Broadway musical.

### Terry Jones:

*Blazing Dragons*, although made for children, is an extremely witty and inventive cartoon series.

*The Crusades*, 1995 documentary that he co-wrote and presented. Yes, Jones is a serious medieval historian.

*Medieval Lives*, recent documentary series in which he plays various roles to bring the period to life.

### Michael Palin:

*Brazil*, where his ability to switch from nice to nasty sends a shiver down the spine.

*Ripping Yarns*, a paean to Boy's Own adventure stories of the 1920s and 1930s.

*GBH*, where the role of Jim Nelson showcased his serious acting abilities.

### Popular UK shows that were remade for the US market:

| UK | US |
| --- | --- |
| *Are You Being Served?* | *Beanes of Boston* |
| *The Fall and Rise of Reginald Perrin* | *Reggie* |
| *Fawlty Towers* | *Amanda's* and *Payne* |
| *Man About the House* | *Three's Company* |
| *Mind Your Language* | *What a Country* |
| *Not the Nine O'Clock News* | *Not Necessarily the News* |
| *On the Buses* | *Lotsa Luck* |
| *One Foot in the Grave* | *Cosby* |
| *Porridge* | *On the Rocks* |
| *Spitting Image* | *D. C. Follies* |
| *Steptoe and Son* | *Sanford and Son* |
| *Till Death Us Do Part* | *All in the Family* |

### And the US shows remade in the UK:

| US | UK |
| --- | --- |
| *Friends* | *Coupling* |
| *The Golden Girls* | *The Brighton Belles* |
| *Good Times* | *The Fosters* |
| *The Larry Sanders Show* | *Bob Martin* |
| *Mad About You* | *Loved by You* |
| *Married . . . with Children* | *Married for Life* |
| *Maude* | *Nobody's Perfect* |
| *That '70s Show* | *Days Like These* |
| *Who's the Boss?* | *The Upper Hand* |

> **Daphne: "Don't tell me that men have never used sex to get what they want."**
> **Frasier: "How can men possibly use sex to get what we want? Sex *is* what we want!"**
> Kelsey Grammer and Jane Leeves in *Frasier*

# Soap suds

FROM GRIM BRITISH REALISM TO GLOSSY
AMERICAN EXCESS

Some soap villains are scoundrels (not to mention killers, rapists and swindlers), while others tease you with their soft side, or practice a kind of honor among thieves, while still terrorizing their neighbors.

1. **Richard Hillman** – *Coronation Street*'s serial killer: "You're Norman Bates with a briefcase!" screeched his wife Gail, when she found out he'd been offing little old ladies.

2. **J. R. Ewing** – The ruthless oil magnate from *Dallas* who'd sell his grandmother for a nickel, given the chance.

3. **Grant Mitchell** – Baldy psycho mechanic on *EastEnders* who, between leaning on people, found time to sleep with his brother's wife and girlfriend, and his pregnant girlfriend's mother as well.

4. **Trevor Jordache** – *Brookside*'s two-faced wife beater who ended up getting battered himself, then buried under the patio.

5. **Nick Cotton** – *EastEnders* reprobate whose dear old mom wanted to forgive him, even when he was poisoning her.

6. **Alexis Colby-Carrington-Dexter** – Undoubtedly queen bitch of the soap opera world, always scheming and seducing on *Dynasty*.

7. **Dennis Watts** – Better known as Dirty Den, *EastEnders*' top innkeeper kept everyone in his manor in order—or else.

8. **Joan "The Freak" Ferguson** – *Prisoner of Cell Block H*'s most sadistic warder was not above murder and sexual assault to get her wicked way.

9. **Kim Tate** – Proving you can be as evil in a Barbour as a shell suit, the *Emmerdale* vixen taunted her sick husband until he had a heart attack then enjoyed watching him die.

10. **Barry Grant** – *Brookside*'s symbol of Thatcherite entrepreneurial spirit gone wrong, Barry wound up murdering his best friend's family.

If anything accounted for the rapid popularity of *EastEnders* during its first few years, it was the violent sparring between Queen Vic landlord "Dirty" Den Watts and his over-made-up wife, Angie. More than thirty million Brits tuned in on Christmas Day, 1986, to watch Den give his wife the ultimate present—divorce papers. With a cheery "Happy Christmas, Ange!" he leaves her to swill gin and weep. The audience was the fourth highest ever recorded for a TV program in the UK, and the highest for a soap opera.

Den was the first character seen when the first episode was aired, and tabloid papers were soon full of actor Leslie Grantham's past exploits—including serving 10 years for a murder committed when he was 19 years old. Grantham had, in fact, first auditioned for the part of Pete Beale, but the producers thought he was too good looking, and gave him the role of Den instead. But by 1989, he had scared and shagged his way through most of the cast, and it was clear writers didn't quite know what to do with him any longer. Cue a mysterious gunman, an off-screen splash as something falls into the local canal, and no more Dirty Den.

Den's dead body was never shown—it was supposedly fished out of the canal a year later—and in 2003, Grantham was tempted back to resurrect one of the soap world's greatest villains, turning up in his daughter Sharon's club with a laconic "'Allo, Princess." Having sold the Queen Vic to Frank Butcher years before his first "death," Den proceeded to buy it back from Sam Mitchell and moved in with his new wife Chrissie, who he didn't always see eye to eye with. By February 2005, she had enough of him, and killed him, a plotline instigated after Grantham's popularity took a nosedive, following tabloid newspaper reports of his habit of masturbating in front of a webcam while being viewed by a woman known only as "Amanda."

**This is the story of two sisters: Jessica Tate and Mary Campbell . . . Confused? You won't be, after tonight's (or this week's) episode of . . . *Soap*.**

Roy Roddy introduced each episode of *Soap* with a recap designed to confuse

# I DON'T BELIEVE IT . . .

Soap operas have a habit of straying into the realms of the unbelievable, then attempting to get themselves back on the straight and narrow with the help of increasingly desperate plot devices.

The long-running soap *Dallas*, which ran for 18 years (13 seasons), became notorious for explaining away the whole of season seven (including the death of popular character Bobbie Ewing, played by Patrick Duffy), as events dreamed by his wife Pam (Victoria Principal).

But perhaps strangest of all was the ending to *Crossroads*, a long-running soap made in the Midlands of England, and set among the staff and guests at a motel. *Crossroads* featured several actors who seemed to find it hard to move and speak at the same time—some also seemed to find English quite difficult—and was often lampooned for its poor production values. Nonetheless it had a vigorous following, and despite being axed in 1988 after 25 years, it was revived in 2001, albeit with only three members of the rather elderly original cast. The show only lasted two years, when in a radical move the final episode revealed that the trials and tribulation of life at a "glamorous" Midlands motel were, in fact, the dream existence of a bunch of downtrodden supermarket staff.

## SOAP'S BIGGEST DRIP?

Most people associate him with J. R.'s nice younger brother, Bobby Ewing, from *Dallas*. But two years before he put on his white Stetson, Patrick Duffy was fighting underwater crime as Mark Harris in *The Man from Atlantis*. With webbed fingers and, well, not much else other than a pair of sparkly Speedos, the mysterious swimmer foiled baddies—generally environmental terrorists and the ongoing arch-villain, Mr. Schubert—from 1976 to 1978. With his futuristic submarine, the *Cetacean*, and an attractive scientist love interest, Dr. Elizabeth Merrill, the Man from Atlantis (supposedly a lone survivor of an ancient and noble race) would often become annoyed at the stupidity of the surface dwellers polluting the beauty of the seas. *The Man from Atlantis* has the distinction of being the first American TV show broadcast in the People's Republic of China. Whether they should have paid more attention to what *Dallas* did to Communism in Romania remains to be seen.

While most soap star singers manage, if they're lucky, a handful of hits, an album that sells to mums at Christmas, and a few gigs opening supermarkets, Kylie Minogue is the only superstar to graduate from the soap circuit.

In the late 1980s, Minogue and Jason Donovan (who looked as though he'd keep up with her until he started losing his hair and *The Face* magazine erroneously accused him of being gay) became the prince and princess of pop on the back of their romantic roles in Aussie soap *Neighbours*.

Kylie churned out a series of Stock, Aitken, and Waterman-produced hits, starting with "I Should Be So Lucky," and bounced around in the accompanying videos in bright but tacky outfits with a mass of ringlets and a sweet pout. This went on into the early 1990s, after which her star began to wane. Several attempts to relaunch the *Neighbours* star as a serious artist failed, but as things turned out, it was just a case of giving people enough time to forget the bubbly, zany Charlene and consider Kylie in her own right as a performer.

In 2000, Kylie returned to the music scene with a string of sophisticated dance floor hits aimed at the coveted "tween" demographic, yet clever enough to inspire remixes from some of the world's best-regarded DJs as well. Making killer videos featuring short shorts and draped dresses that looked like they'd fall off any moment (or so people hoped) didn't hurt either.

Kylie has managed to score Number 1 hits in 45 countries, proving her truly universal appeal. She's had 28 top 10 singles in the UK, second only to Madonna among female artists. And though her fellow Aussies once turned up their noses at her music, she now holds the record for the largest number of concert tickets sold there, and has had nine Number 1s in the Australian singles chart. Even these sales are just a drop in the ocean, however, when you consider her worldwide sales: 40 million singles and 25 million albums.

When it comes to longevity, US soaps have all the others beaten, with many entering their *fifth decade*! Here's a round-up of the soaps that survived 10 years or more.

*Guiding Light* (1937–1955 on radio, 1952–present on television)

*Love of Life* (1951–1980)

*Search for Tomorrow* (1951–1986)

*The Secret Storm* (1954–1974)

*As the World Turns* (1956–present)

*The Edge of Night* (1956–1984)

*General Hospital* (1963–present)

*The Doctors* (1963–1982)

*Another World* (1964–1999)

*Days of Our Lives* (1965–present)

*One Life to Live* (1968–present)

*All My Children* (1970–present)

*The Young and the Restless* (1973–present)

*Ryan's Hope* (1975–1989)

*Dallas* (1978–1991)

*Knots Landing* (1979–1993)

*Beverly Hills 90210* (1990–2000)

*Loving* (1983–1995)

## GHOULIES AND GHOSTIES AND LONG-LEGGED BEASTIES . . .

Back in June 1966, the ABC network began showing a soap with a difference: *Dark Shadows*. In addition to the usual romantic complications and emotional crises, the inhabitants of Collinsport, Maine also had to contend with a number of mysteries that were positively gothic. With these overtones of H. P. Lovecraft, the early storylines merely hinted at dark family secrets among the fisher folk. The show made extensive use of flashbacks to suggest the past haunting the present, sometimes devoting whole episodes to a past event, but after a couple of years the ratings began to fall. At this point executive producer Dan Curtis's children made a suggestion: stop hinting and actually introduce supernatural characters. By the time the show was cancelled in 1971, all sorts of bizarre characters had appeared, a parallel timeline had been established, and the characters had traveled to 1995.

Curtis introduced Josette Collins as a spectral ancestor of the central family, and had her save them from a deranged killer (Matthew Morgan). He followed up the angelic watchdog with an undying demon posing as an estranged wife (Laura Murdoch Collins), an unwilling vampire (Barnabas Collins), and a very sexy witch (Angelique). But it was the brooding Quentin Collins, played by David Selby, that many fans remember most fondly. Quentin is slowly revealed to be a werewolf in a massive flashback sequence that lasted from March 3, 1969 to January 6, 1970—a total of more than 10 months!

The show remains extremely popular to this day: in the US regular conventions attract thousands of followers, and British sci-fi fans eagerly seek episode tapes—even though the series has never been shown in the UK.

Spoofing soap operas clichés is rather like shooting fish in a barrel, and many shows have had a go. But two US shows did it magnificently well:

*Mary Hartman, Mary Hartman* (often abbreviated to *MH2*) dealt with the same melodramatic topics as ordinary daytime soaps. But the show talked openly, rather than obliquely, about subjects such as homosexuality, impotence, and sexual perversions, leading many TV stations to broadcast it only after 11pm. The first episode featured a family being murdered and introduced the "Fernwood Flasher," who turned out to be Mary Hartman's grandpa.

*Soap* was even madder. It mixed well-known actors (such as Katherine Helmond as the deliciously airheaded Jessica Tate) with existing soap stars, and gave a big break to the young Billy Crystal, who played primetime's first cheerfully homosexual character, Jodie. That aside, many stations got upset over a plotline involving a character's affair with a Roman Catholic priest, not to mention a schoolboy's affair with his teacher, and an interracial romance.

The UK's best soap spoof is undoubtedly Victoria Wood's *Acorn Antiques*, which parodies the cheap production values of *Crossroads*. Episodes appeared as part of *Victoria Wood As Seen On TV* from 1985 to 1987, and featured a lovingly observed variety of missed cues, misplaced props, poor continuity, and fluffed lines.

> I was out of work and got two scripts that same day. One was for a sitcom called *The Waverly Wonders*, which Joe Namath eventually got. The other was *Dallas*. I called my agent and said, "Let's go with *Dallas*." And he said, "You're crazy. That thing is never going to go."
> Larry Hagman recalls the best hunch of his life

## TELEVISION NOVELS

Up until the launch of *Peyton Place* in 1964, most successful American soap operas were daytime viewing. *Peyton Place* was an altogether more adult, and complicated, affair, at one point boasting over one hundred regular cast members intricately involved with each other. Adapted from a potboiler by Norah Lofts, which had been filmed successfully in 1957, it was termed a "television novel" because the writer, Paul Monash, hated the term soap opera.

The first episode featured Mia Farrow as Allison MacKenzie, niece of the newspaper editor in the quiet town of Peyton Place, falling in love with Ryan O'Neal, who played the elder brother of one of her classmates—a relationship her mother disapproved of. Farrow left the series in 1966 following her marriage to Frank Sinatra, but her character's presence was maintained. Leigh Taylor-Young, playing a mysterious woman, turns up with Allison's bracelet— Taylor-Young would go on to romance and marry Ryan O'Neal in real life. Then Joyce Jillson arrives as Jill Smith, claiming to be raising Allison's baby. Many years later, the character of Elliot Carson would be written into the series; he was supposedly Allison's father and his unexpected appearance was explained by the fact that he had been in jail.

*Peyton Place* was one of the first shows to encourage major screen actors to join a soap for a season or two, and over the years it attracted Gena Rowlands, Susan Oliver, and Lee Grant, as well as featuring Wilfred Hyde-White. It was regarded as classier than your average soap opera, and even though it only lasted six years, has long been remembered as the ultimate soap.

*Dallas* contributed to the downfall of the Communist government in Romania. No, really, it did: In the 1980s, Nicolae Ceausescu's government decided to show episodes of Dallas on state television (whose schedules were mostly filled by footage of Ceausescu giving speeches on how good he was to his people). They picked the show because, to them, it epitomised the evil consumerism of the West with its villainous characters cheating and scheming for money and power. However, Romanian viewers paid less attention to the plots and more to the lavish homes, clothes, restaurants, and cars; and they liked what they saw. As Larry Hagman pointed out in an interview, they wanted to know "Why don't we have that over here?" and promptly "took old Ceausescu and his wife out and shot them both 500 times."

The show was so popular that following the overthrow of Communism, a Romanian billionaire built a replica of Southfork, the Ewing's Dallas ranch, in Hermes Land, Slobazia, and opened it as a theme park.

Another politically sensitive soap is BBC Radio 4's *The Archers*. Apparently the version of the show broadcast in Pakistani was so popular in Afghanistan before the US invasion that keen listeners ignored the Taliban's ban on foreign broadcasts to illegally tune in to the doings of simple country folk in Ambridge.

> **The level of misery in *EastEnders* has long been a standing joke; Dante himself would have blanched at the unrelenting suffering produced by the beatings, shootings, extramarital affairs (ideally with your husband's brother or mother's boyfriend), abortions, addictions, rapes, overdoses, debts, and false imprisonments.**
>
> Lucy Mangan identifies what kept the show ahead
> in the ratings in *The Guardian*

# Watching the detectives

## FROM GRITTY COPS TO GERIATRIC SLEUTHS

*The Streets of San Francisco* is remembered by many fans as one of the best cop dramas ever made. It teamed a widowed veteran detective who worked his way up the force the hard way (Mike Stone, played by the nasally prominent Karl Malden) with a smart, hip young detective (Steve Keller, played by dimple-chinned Michael Douglas). Both were strong actors and developed the intrinsic tension between their mismatched characters and styles of policing well.

Douglas, whose character dressed very fashionably, became a sex symbol, while Malden became a tough-guy icon. Running from 1972 until 1977, the series came from the same production team that gave us *Hawaii Five-O*, and made much of its West Coast location, using actual San Francisco Police Department buildings, including the city morgue.

Things began to go wrong when Douglas left the show in 1975 to pursue a film career, and was replaced by Richard Hatch (who went on to play Apollo from *Battlestar Galactica*). Unfortunately, it seemed that acting was not Hatch's strong suit. As one fan commented: "Richard Hatch redefined stiffness. Quinn and Martin (the show's producers) may have had as much success if they paired Malden up with a mannequin from the men's department at Macy's with sound dubbing, rather than putting Hatch on the payroll." After just one season with Hatch, the show was cancelled.

> **Never accept an invitation to a country house weekend if Hercule Poirot is staying in the neighborhood, on account of the man being a lightning rod for murder.**
>
> Joe Joseph points out the unlikelihood of famous sleuths ever having a social life, as people drop dead wherever they go, in *The Times*

# WHAT'S IN A NAME?

For many years *Columbo* fans believed that Lieutenant Columbo's first name, which is never mentioned in the series, was Philip. But the advent of DVD has revealed that on his police identification it says Frank. In "Dead Weight," his signature can clearly be read when you can see a close-up of his badge as he shows it to General Hollister.

Perhaps the reason so many people believe Columbo's first name is Philip is that it says so in *The Trivia Encyclopedia*, compiled by Fred L. Worth. He invented this to prove that people were infringing his copyright and, as he suspected, it was widely copied by other writers.

In 1984, Worth filed an unsuccessful $300 million lawsuit against the distributors of the board game Trivial Pursuit, claiming that they had sourced their questions from his books; even to the point of reproducing misprints and typographical errors. The ace up his sleeve was "Philip Columbo," which appeared in a game question, despite the name being an invention of his.

Trivial Pursuit did not deny they sourced material from Worth's books (among others) and submitted that copying from a single source is plagiarism, but compiling information from several sources is called research. The judge agreed, ruling in favor of the company, and the case was promptly thrown out of court.

## REASONS *COP ROCK* WAS DREADFUL

1. Although the songs progressed the storylines, they were all over the place, spirituals one minute, unfortunate rap numbers the next.

2. Quite a lot of the leading parts were taken by people who were, at best, indifferent singers.

3. Each episode cost $1.8m dollars, a record high for a TV show at the time.

4. William L. Finkelstein co-produced. He's a great writer (*Murder One*, *NYPD Blue*, *Law & Order*, *L.A. Law*) but not a great co-creator.

5. It's got Barbara Bosson (Mrs. Bochco) in it . . . again . . .

# LADY COPS

If you think patrolling the mean streets is no job for a woman you may get a surprise. Ever alert for a novel twist, program creators on both sides of the Atlantic have produced a surprisingly large number of cop shows with female leads. Here are some of the groundbreakers:

1. *The Gentle Touch* (1980–1984) – Maggie Forbes fights hard for respect in the testosterone-heavy British police force.

2. *Cats' Eyes* (1985–1987) – Jill Gasgoine recruits a couple of female assistants to open the Eyes Enquiry Agency, after leaving the police at the end of *The Gentle Touch*.

3. *Juliet Bravo* (1980–1985) – Stephanie Turner, then Anna Cartaret, played the tough detective inspectors policing the fictional northern English town of Hartley.

4. *Cagney & Lacey* (1982–1988) – Unusual for showing female cops as both tough and sexy (Sharon Gless) and warm and maternal (Tyne Daly).

5. *Dempsey & Makepeace* (1985–1987) – US–UK, male-female team cop show in which American maverick James Dempsey finds himself sleuthing in the UK with a female detective sergeant.

6. *Prime Suspect* (1991) – Revolutionary Lynda La Plante series about Detective Jane Tennison, played by Helen Mirren as a fragile yet determined woman in charge of a hostile and macho homicide unit.

## REASONS *COP ROCK* WASN'T AS BAD AS ALL THAT

1. It was created by Stephen Bochco, the man who gave us the most influential police drama ever created, *Hill Street Blues*.

2. It was a brave idea before its time: police procedural meets Broadway show.

3. Oscar-winning composer Randy Newman led the songwriting team required to provide several numbers for each hour-long episode.

4. It's got C. C. H. Pounder in it, one of the most entertaining African-American actresses around.

5. It's not nearly as bad as *Hull High*, the other musical drama that debuted in 1990, set in a high school.

For many people there is only one cop show. It is the Ur-show, the source from which all later cop shows are drawn. Its influence cannot be escaped, cannot be avoided. Once Steven Bochco's *Hill Street Blues* debuted in 1981, cops on TV would never be the same again.

*Hill Street Blues*, known simply as *The Hill* to many fans, revolutionized how people viewed the police. Many of the show's characters were heroic, but there were no actual heroes—just nuanced, flawed, realistically drawn characters—and no grandstanding. They were ordinary (and very ordinary-looking) people trying to do a hard job under difficult conditions, from the gangs on the streets to the overflowing stationhouse toilets.

Bochco dramatized the structure of a police department with its petty rivalries, grudges, unspoken friendships, and sudden horrors. Everything looked worn, every scene was chaotic, with people talking over each other, blocking the cameras. The point of view never stayed in the same place, either visually or morally, as Captain Frank Furillo (the brilliant Daniel J. Travanti) struggled to keep his staff motivated while dealing with the nightmare bureaucracy around him. And week by week, its huge ensemble cast seemed to become part of your family.

Because it went on so long with no drop in standards (it won three Golden Globes and 25 Emmys), and because it had such a varied cast, the writers could show multiple sides of each character. Every episode showed the events of a single day, and no matter how dramatic those might be, you always got a rounded picture of life in a police precinct.

Writers on the series included David Milch, who went on to create HBO's *Deadwood*, as well as co-creating *NYPD Blue* with Bochco; Dick Wolf, now king of the *Law & Order* franchise; Mark Frost, who co-created *Twin Peaks* with David Lynch, and playwright David Mamet. Alan Rachins, who also wrote for the series, is perhaps more familiar as the much put-upon Douglas Brackman in *L.A. Law*— and he happens to be Bochco's brother-in-law.

Originally Lieutenant Columbo (first name Frank, inspired by Porfiry Petrovich in Dostoyevsky's *Crime and Punishment*) appeared as a supporting character in the NBC anthology series *The Chevy Mystery Show*, played by Bert Freed. He then appeared in a stage play, *Prescription*, before finally getting his own show in 1971. Over its run (specials were still being made as late as 2003), the show attracted a huge range of guest stars: everyone from Shakespearean actors to country singers. Unlike most detective shows, the guest star was always the murderer, and audiences almost always saw them do it right from the start. The tension was created by how Columbo would manage to finally book them. Here are just a few of the famous killers:

Johnny Cash ● John Cassavetes ● Billy Connolly
Robert Culp (three times, sporting different moustaches!)
Tyne Daly ● Faye Dunaway ● Dick Van Dyke
José Ferrer ● Louis Jourdan ● Martin Landau
Janet Leigh ● Ida Lupino ● Roddy McDowall
Patrick McGoohan (four times) ● Ray Milland
Leonard Nimoy ● Donald Pleasence
William Shatner (twice) ● Robert Vaughn

British detective fiction was always a vehicle for social retribution. It allows the middle class to dismiss the other two classes for what they are: the same, and not us. Like the undeserving poor, the nobs don't work, spend money irresponsibly, can't control their sexual appetites and are indifferent to the many children they foist on the rest of us, who have to be sexually responsible and work for a living. It's satisfying to see a few of them die of unnatural causes, and if the detective who delivers their comeuppance comes from one class or the other, all the better.

*New York Times* TV critic Alessandra Stanley on classic British murder mysteries

# A DIFFERENT KIND OF POLICE

*Hawaii Five-O* was a Technicolor wonder, bringing the exotic into the American living room. It featured Jack Lord as Steve McGarrett, a laid-back leader who headed a team of sharply-dressed (and in some cases quite rotund) locals, including Kam Fong as Detective Chin Ho Kelly, who really had been a policeman (and an estate agent) before turning to acting.

McGarrett had a habit of calling his team by nicknames like Kimo, Duke, and Big Kanaka—and of course Danny Williams became "Danno of Book 'em, Danno!" fame. The only episode where McGarrett actually booked the suspect himself was "A Death in the Family," when he had just arrested Chin Ho Kelly's murderer.

Lord's role had originally been offered to Gregory Peck, who turned it down. Lord had been considered for the role of Captain James T. Kirk in *Star Trek* in 1966, but wanted to be involved in producing it, which Gene Roddenberry wouldn't agree to it. That left him free to take on the role of McGarrett, which he would occupy from 1968 until 1980.

By the time the series ended, Jack Lord was looking quite infirm. He only made one more appearance, as Admiral Henderson in the 1980 TV movie *M Station: Hawaii*, which he also directed, and after that stayed out of the limelight until his death in 1998, at age 77.

## THE WORST DETECTIVE SHOW THAT NEVER WAS

Get down on your knees, lift your arms in supplication to whatever god you pray to, and thank them that even the might of the Walt Disney Corporation couldn't get a stinker like the *Turner & Hooch* TV show off the ground.

A pilot was filmed in 1990, a year after Tom Hanks had failed to impress anyone with his performance as a young detective partnered with a drooling bloodhound. He was replaced in the series that never was by Tom Wilson, best known for his performance as Biff Tannen in the *Back to the Future* movies. Executives Michael Eisner and Jeffrey Katzenberg had tried to induce the then-unknown Tim Allen to take on that part, and also the lead in a small-screen version of *Dead Poets Society*, both of which he wisely declined. Instead, he persuaded them to commission *Home Improvement*, based around his stand-up routine *Men Are Pigs*.

## THERE'S A TIME AND A PLACE FOR MURDER

Although the majority of their subjects seem to die in casinos, clubs and the desert, in *CSI* the characters are asked to investigate dead bodies in some very strange places including:

A hotel hosting a dwarf convention

The closed jury room of a murder trial

The undercarriage of a bus

An S&M brothel ● Area 51

A 120-mile relay race course ● An airliner in flight

A word-game tournament

A traveling carnival ● A crop circle

A state mental hospital ● A Buddhist temple

A tree in the forest with a scuba diver wedged in it

A secret playroom full of adult-sized baby equipment

A convention for people who like to dress up as giant furry animals, known as Furries (which is, by the way, a real-life phenomenon)

## DICKS WITH TICKS

In an effort to make them stand out from the crowd, writers and producers give their detectives a shtick, whether it's the car they drive, the clothes they wear, or their funny little habits . . . For a while in the 1960s and 1970s, every American cop or private eye seemed to require a notable gimmick or quirk:

*Cannon* (debuted 1971) – the fat detective, played by William Conrad

*Ironside* (debuted 1967) – the detective in a wheelchair, played by Raymond Burr

*Kojak* (debuted 1973) – the bald detective with a lollipop, played by Telly Savalas

*Longstreet* (debuted 1971) – the blind detective, played by James Franciscus

*McCloud* (debuted 1970) – the cowboy detective, played by Dennis Weaver

*Monk* (debuted 2002) – the detective with obsessive compulsive disorder, played by Tony Shalhoub

*Tenafly* (debuted 1973) – the gentle black detective, played by James McEachin

## BOOM AND BUST

Graham Yost cut his teeth writing screenplays for fast-moving films like 1994's *Speed* and 1996's *Broken Arrow*. He applied both skill and slickness when he created his first (and so far, only) TV show, having written scripts, and produced and directed, for many others.

*Boomtown* was clearly a writer's show. From the very first episode, it featured a massive gimmick, showing and reshowing the same activity from several points of view, stopping and starting at different places, slowly building up a picture of what was happening, jumping about the timeline and really making the audience work to keep up.

Set in Los Angeles, it mixed cop characters with justice department figures (including the compelling Neil McDonough as an alcoholic deputy district attorney, a flawed Machiavellian figure fighting his inner demons as well as his boss), medics and firefighters, and often told the lawbreaker's story, too. Although a bit of a challenge to spoon-fed audiences, the scripts themselves were always things of beauty, with strong characterization—few scripts make stupid characters seem rich and interesting, even if dumb—all the time prodding and poking at the events until the truth shook loose.

The second and final season, in 2003, was a bit less polished than the first, but maintained the intense characterization and surprising denouements that had marked the first season as a truly original, exceptional police drama.

**Here's a selection of the stars who have sleuthed their way through some of Christie's best-loved characters:**

**Hercule Poirot**, Belgian detective extraordinaire, has been played by:
David Suchet (on TV)
*. . . and on film:*
Austin Trevor
Albert Finney
Peter Ustinov
Tony Randall
Alfred Molina

**Miss Marple**, easily overlooked little old lady detective, has been played by:
Gracie Fields (US TV)
Margaret Rutherford (TV movies)
Angela Lansbury (film)
Helen Hayes (TV)
Joan Hickson (TV)
June Whitefield (radio)
Geraldine McEwan (TV)

**Tommy and Tuppence**, adventurous young blackmailers turned detective:
James Warwick and Francesca Annis (TV)

The Nippon Housou Kyoukai studio in Japan have also created a series called *Great Detectives Poirot and Marple* with animated versions of Christie's characters, and a crime-solving duck called Oliver.

---

**I don't think you can really make television based on what you think audiences want. You can only make stories that you like, because you have to watch it so many times.**

**Dick Wolf, creator of the *Law & Order* franchise**

---

# Go west!

WHEN GOOD GUYS WORE WHITE HATS AND
CRAVED A WILD FRONTIER

*Rawhide* was one of the few TV westerns that wasn't about land: most similar shows display, at their heart, the desire of settlers to make a new and better home for themselves in hostile and forbidding circumstances. They revolve around the premise that even the quietest, most peaceful man can be stirred to action when someone threatens home and family. *Rawhide* concentrates on an eternal cattle drive, and the men who keep the huge herds in motion.

The show began in 1959 with Eric Fleming playing Gil Favor, the trail boss, who is helped by his number two, Rowdy Yates, famously played by the young Clint Eastwood—who stayed with the series until it ended in 1966, yet also found the time to make the trilogy of spaghetti westerns for Sergio Leone that established him as a star in the "moody sonofabitch" mold: *A Fistful of Dollars*, *For a Few Dollars More*, and *The Good, the Bad and the Ugly*.

*Rawhide* quickly established itself as a gritty drama that relied on strong characterization, rather than episodic adventure, to draw viewers in. Set just after the Civil War, it portrayed some of the hardships of life in the saddle as the drovers take their cattle through a landscape devastated by the war. In early episodes the cowboys often encountered not bad guys, but much greater threats such as epidemics, poisoned wells, and drought.

**The Lone Ranger:** "Only you, Tonto, know I'm alive. To the world, I'm buried here beside my brother and my friends . . . forever."
**Tonto:** "You are alone now. Last man. You are lone ranger."
**The Lone Ranger:** "Yes, Tonto, I am . . . the Lone Ranger."

How the Lone Ranger got his name, after the rest of his troop of rangers was killed

## LONGEST-RUNNING WESTERN SERIES

Gunsmoke

Lassie

Bonanza

The Virginian

Cheyenne

The Lone Ranger

Rawhide

Adventures of Wild Bill Hickok

Have Gun, Will Travel

Wagon Train

## WHEN THE CHIPS ARE DOWN . . .

In the late 1950s, American viewers were wooed and won over by a family of sweet-talking, fast-shooting gamblers, known as the Mavericks. First there were just Bret and Bart, played by James Garner and Jack Kelly, but in the fourth season the pair were joined by English cousin Beauregarde, played by Roger Moore with all his customary stiffness. The show was known for its witty scripts, especially Bret's aphorisms, which always began, "As my old Pappy used to say . . ."

*Maverick* ran from 1957 to 1962, but Garner left the show after the third series in 1960, and sued Warner Brothers for breach of contract because they had suspended him without pay during a writers' strike that year, claiming there were no scripts available to film. In court Garner's lawyers showed that Warner Brothers had in fact obtained over 100 scripts during the strike, and Garner was released from his contract.

The producers dealt with losing their best-loved character by writing revolving story lines featuring more members of the Maverick clan, before introducing Robert Colvert as Brent Maverick in 1961.

## CHAPS AND CHAPARRALS

Chaps, the leather coverings cowboys wore over their trousers, weren't created to reduce the rubbing effects of sitting in a hard leather saddle all day, as many people imagine. Sometimes they were worn for warmth—as in the hairy chaps you sometimes see, made of angora wool pelt, known as woolies—but chiefly their function was to protect the legs from bush and scrub. "Chap" is a truncation of the Mexican word *chaparreras*.

Chaparrals, after which *The High Chaparral* is named, are harsh hot, dry areas, mostly found in coastal regions (the series was set in Arizona, so go figure). Temperatures in Chaparral regions often reach 104° Fahrenheit, and such locations are often used by filmmakers wanting to do Wild West scenes.

> **Storywise it wasn't very different from what we'd been doing with *Bonanza*.**
> Lorne Greene on *Battlestar Galactica*

## ONE MAN AND HIS HORSE

| | |
|---|---|
| Lone Ranger | Silver |
| Tonto | Scout |
| Roy Rogers | Trigger |
| The Range Rider | Rawhide |
| Zorro | Phantom and Tornado |
| Wild Bill Hickok | Buckshot |
| Jingles (his sidekick) | Joker |
| Tex Ritter | White Flash |
| Gene Autry | Champion |
| Buffalo Bill, Jr. | Chief |
| Bat Masterson | Stardust |
| Hopalong Cassidy | Topper |
| Paladin | Rafter |

During its 10-year run of 249 90-minute episodes, *The Virginian* introduced many supporting characters and special guest stars to enliven the show, and it became something of a tradition to see which Hollywood actor had been tempted to do a cameo each week. In order of appearance, viewers were treated to:

Ricardo Montalban – *The Big Deal*
George C. Scott – *The Brazen Bell*
Aldo Ray – *Big Day, Great Day, Jacob Was a Plain Man*
Lee Marvin – *It Tolls for Thee*
Bette Davis – *The Accomplice*
Fabian – *Say Goodbye to All That, Two Men Named Laredo, Outcast*
Ida Lupino – *A Distant Fury, We've Lost a Train*
Ed Asner – *Echo of Another Day*
Joan Blondell – *To Make This Place Remember*
Broderick Crawford – *A Killer in Town*
Robert Redford – *The Evil That Men Do*
Ryan O'Neal – *It Takes a Big Man*
Slim Pickens – *Run Quiet, Big Image . . . Little Man*
Yvonne De Carlo – *A Time Remembered*
DeForest Kelley and Leonard Nimoy – *Man of Violence*
Bruce Dern – *First to Thine Own Self, The Payment*
Leslie Nielsen – *Ryker, The Fortress*
Robert Culp – *The Stallion*
Kurt Russell – *A Father for Toby, The Brothers*
Adam West – *Legend for a Lawman*
William Shatner – *The Claim*
Charles Bronson – *Nobility of Kings, Reckoning*
Leonard Nimoy – *Show Me a Hero*
Telly Savalas – *Men with Guns*
John Cassavetes – *Long Ride to Wind River*
Angie Dickinson, Warren Oates – *Ride to Delphi*
Harrison Ford – *The Modoc Kid*
Joan Collins – *The Lady from Wichita*
Patrick Macnee – *A King's Ransom*

Over the years there have been a number of futuristic Westerns. Some, like *The Wild Wild West*, crossed scientifically advanced ideas with a traditional Western setting, while others had all the trappings of sci-fi adventures but are, at heart, just Westerns with space ships instead of wagons, and aliens instead of Indians.

*The Wild Wild West*, which inspired the 1999 Will Smith movie, was commissioned when the Western's domination of TV schedules was beginning to wane. Between 1965 and 1970, Robert Conrad played James T. West, a special agent of President Grant, whose weekly task was to defeat the forces of evil, whether revolutionaries, anarchist bombers or simple criminals. West was assisted by Artemus Gordon, master of disguise, and travelled around in a railroad car, stuffed with futuristic gizmos to help the pair defeat the bad guys.

Another show in a similar vein was 1982's *Q.E.D.*, which was much more H. G. Wells than Wells Fargo. Professor Deverill was a whiz at knocking together useful gadgets for sleuthing, which helped him defeat the evil Dr. Kilkiss, a mad scientist bent on taking over the world, aided by his slightly bumbling butler, Phipps.

One of the most inventive sci-fi Westerns, though short-lived, was *Outlaws*, which ran from 1986-87 on CBS. The pilot shows Sheriff John Grail about to capture a gang of bank robbers in 1899. Grail is struck by lightning, and finds that both he and the gang have been transported through time to 1989. The nineteenth-century cowboys find that standards have slipped, and set about righting wrongs wearing cowboy outfits hired from a costume shop, and using six shooters.

*The Secret Empire* (known as *Cliffhangers: The Secret Empire* in the US) also featured time travel. The show only lasted part of one season in 1979, possibly because its habit of switching between black and white scenes set in the Wild West, and futuristic color ones set in the underground city of Chimera, just confused viewers.

Some of the most successful hybrids have simply taken the plot and pacing of a Western and substituted ray guns and silver suits. Joss Whedon's *Firefly*, is essentially *The Outlaw Josey Wales* in space, and *Battlestar Galactica*, once you take away the fighters and religious imagery, is *Wagon Train* all over again. (Producer Glen A. Larson even described it that way in pitch meetings for the show.)

The city of Deadwood, South Dakota, was founded during a gold rush in 1875. HBO's popular modern reworking of the cowboy show, the amoral and shocking *Deadwood*, features many characters based on actual historical figures:

**Al Swerengen**, (played by Ian McShane in the series), was the owner of the Gem Theater (as taverns with hookers were euphemistically called) who used women he'd lured to the town with promises of more legitimate work, then turned into whores. At his peak Swerengen was said to take in $10,000 a night at the Gem, but he died penniless.

**Dan Dority** (or Doherty) was Swerengen's general manager and Johnny Burns was his "box handler"—in charge of the prostitutes. Both were known as violent men who beat the women in their charge.

**Seth Bullock** and **Sol Star** were also real figures in Deadwood's history, but only arrived in Deadwood the day before Wild Bill Hickok was shot, so never became friends with him. They'd already run a hardware firm in Montana, and came to Deadwood in search of gold, not increased shovel sales. They moved into ranching and Star went on to be Mayor of Deadwood for 14 years.

**E. B. Farnum** was, in fact, a pillar of the Deadwood community. Not only was he elected as Mayor, he went on to sit on the town's first School Board, organized the building of the Deadwood to Centennial toll road that secured the camp's supply routes, and was a Justice of the Peace.

The real **Reverend Henry Smith** had been a doctor in the Civil War and was an itinerant preacher in Deadwood. He was found dead by the roadside, killed by an Indian, having set out to walk to nearby Crook City to minister to the people there.

**Calamity Jane** was a foulmouthed, liquor-loving woman, much as shown in the series. She always claimed to have been Hickok's lover, and had previously worked as a nurse, prostitute and army scout before arriving at the camp.

**"Crooked Nose" Jack McCall** was tried for the murder of Wild Bill Hickok in McDaniels' Theatre in August, 1976. According to the local newspaper, *The Traveller*: "His head, which is covered by a thick crop of chestnut hair, is very narrow as to the parts occupied by the intellectual portion of the brain, while the animal development is exceedingly large. The nose is what is commonly called 'snub,' cross eyes, and a florid complexion, and the picture is finished."

**Wild Bill Hickok**, according to *The Traveller*, had a reputation for gunplay that "was very hard; he was quick in using the pistol and never missed his man, and had killed quite a number of persons in different parts of the country."

**Charlie Utter** had been a friend of Wild Bill for many years before they arrived in Deadwood. The real Utter, like his fictional counterpart, went on to open a transportation business after his friend's death.

**Mr. Hearst**, the mysterious developer on whose behalf the fictitious Francis Wolcott acts, did exist—he was the father of newspaper magnate William Randolph Hearst, on whom *Citizen Kane* was based.

**The Metz family** were attacked and murdered on the road from Deadwood to Laramie, and the slaughter was initially blamed on Indians then found to be the work of white raiders. But there were no children in the party.

---

**We took our men from Texas, Kentucky, and Virginia; from the mountains and the backwoods and the plains. We put them under orders—guerrilla fighting orders, and what we lacked in numbers, we made up in speed and brains. Both Rebs and Yankee strangers, they called us "Mosby's Rangers." Both North and South they knew our fame. Gray Ghost is what they called me; John Mosby is my name.**

Opening narration to the unusual *Gray Ghost* series, based on a real-life Civil War guerilla leader, Major John Singleton Mosby

---

Apart from the rather robust, tub-thumping sound of the Bonanza orchestra, most Western shows chose a nice lyrical ballad as their theme tune. The Rebel was lucky enough to get Johnny Cash to sing its less than inspired theme song, which didn't even rhyme: "Johnny Yuma, was a rebel / He roamed, through the west / And Johnny Yuma, was a rebel / He wandered alone." A quick survey shows that neither rhyme, rhythm nor reason are well-represented in this musical genre:

*Sugarfoot* – known as *Tenderfoot* in the UK
"Sugarfoot, Sugarfoot, easy lopin', cattle ropin' Sugarfoot
Carefree as the tumbleweeds, a joggin' along with a heart full of song
And a rifle and a volume of the law."

*Bat Masterson* – struggling for a rhyme for the name
"Back when the West was very young
There lived a man named Masterson."

"And those with too handy a trigger
Forgot to figure
On his fighting cane."

*Bronco* – what the hell, let's just repeat the name again
"Bronco, Bronco, tearin' across the Texas plain
Bronco, Bronco, Bronco Layne."

*Have Gun Will Travel* – more problems finding rhymes for the name
"His fast gun for hire heeds the calling wind
A soldier of fortune is the man called Paladin."

*Jim Bowie* – and more repeating of the name
"Jim Bowie! Jim Bowie!
He was a fighter, a fearless, and mighty adventurin' man!"

*Rawhide* – just in case you have a tendency to psychoanalyze your dinner
"Don't try to understand 'em / Just rope 'em, pull and brand 'em."

*Yancy Derringer* – how many manor houses were there in the
old West, exactly?
"They sing of Yancy Derringer
On every danger trail
On riverboat, in manor house."

*Wyatt Earp* – sometimes you can have too much rhyme
"The West it was lawless / But one man was flawless."

## ALIAS BUTCH AND SUNDANCE

Two years after the success of *Butch Cassidy and the Sundance Kid*, the TV movie *Alias Smith and Jones* proved that audiences still had an appetite for easygoing comedy Westerns, and before long the pilot turned into a series. The show starred two fresh-faced actors: Ben Murphy as Jed "Kid" Curry and Pete Duel as Hannibal Heyes, who used the aliases Thadeus Jones and Hannibal Smith because they were wanted for murder. Wrongly accused, Curry and Heyes were offered a deal by the government, and every episode saw them trying to undertake some mission for their paymasters while avoiding the lawmen who were always on their tail.

For all its popularity, the series lasted only two and a half seasons, because Pete Duel killed himself in mysterious circumstances on December 31, 1971, after an evening of heavy drinking. He was known to have had drinking problems in the past, had tried Alcoholics Anonymous several times, and had his driver's license revoked. In an interview six weeks earlier, Duel had said of his character: "He is hunted by every posse, yet he is still able to laugh. It's something I love him for. I try to be like that, but with so many problems besetting the world, from war to pollution and injustice, I find it difficult to keep smiling." The official verdict was "probable suicide."

Roger Davis took over the Hannibal Heyes role (he'd previously been the show's narrator) but fans deserted in droves, and a third season was never finished. To this day fans continue to write new episodes of the show that never happened and post their scripts online. *Alias Smith and Jones* is also one of the favorite subjects of 'slash' fiction—stories that involve a sexual (usually homosexual) relationship between the two leads.

# Space is ace

ALIEN WORLDS THAT MESMERIZE US

## TOP 10 SCI-FI TV CREATORS

Sci-fi television has been one of the best creative outlets for those looking to tell a story and create fascinating worlds and characters for decades. However, each of those TV shows had to have a brilliant mind behind them, driving them and innovating one of the most intelligent genres of TV. Here are the most influential people to ever make sci-fi TV:

1. **Rod Serling** (*The Twilight Zone*)

2. **Gene Roddenberry** (*Star Trek, Andromeda, Earth: Final Conflict*)

3. **Sydney Newman** (*Doctor Who, The Avengers*)

4. **Nigel Kneale** (*Quatermass*)

5. **Terry Nation** (*Doctor Who, Blake's 7, The Survivors*)

6. **Glen A. Larson** (*Battlestar Galactica, Buck Rogers, Knight Rider*)

7. **Joss Whedon** (*Buffy, Angel, Firefly*)

8. **Chris Carter** (*The X-Files, Millennium*)

9. **J. J. Abrams** (*Alias, Lost*)

10. **J. Michael Straczynski** (*Babylon 5, Crusade*)

## THE SAUCY WORLD OF JACQUELINE PEARCE

Before Mulder and Scully, sci-fi fans had another on-off relationship to ponder in the form of *Blake's 7*'s Avon and Servalan. He was a not very good goodie, and she was an extremely bad baddie, and sometimes it seemed one or other would forget which side they were on.

Played by Royal Academy of Dramatic Arts and Actor's Studio graduate Jacqueline Pearce, Servalan's cropped black hair and trademark clinging dresses—no one seemed to question her decision to break out the ballgowns even when landing on hostile planets—were extremely popular with viewers, especially young male ones. To this day she revels in the fact that she's been a "masturbatory fantasy for an entire generation of young men. And still am. Isn't that wonderful? I'm so proud of that. It's a lovely thing to think of yourself playing such a crucial part of a young man's development."

> **Now kindly cluck off, before I extract your gibblets, and shove a large seasoned onion between the lips you never kiss with.**
>
> Chris Barry as Rimmer in *Red Dwarf*; the show was notorious for getting away with almost swearing, often using the term "smeg" from smegma

## "I DON'T KNOW WHAT EGO MEANS"

William Shatner might have indeed believed that, but many of the people he worked with on *Star Trek* disagreed. "Bill has a big fat head," claimed co-star James Doohan, but Leonard Nimoy has always been more diplomatic, saying only, "Sometimes, there was conflict."

Over the years, in interviews his co-stars reported that he got jealous, especially when Nimoy got more fan mail; demanded other characters lines and scenes be cut when he thought Kirk wasn't getting enough exposure in an episode; insisted on being served lunch before everyone else; and was always chasing attractive female extras in his wig and corset. Here's what some of his fellow space thespians had to say about him.

**James Doohan (Scotty):** "There is only one person in the show that nobody can stand . . . He can't even act. He just makes faces."

**George Takei (Sulu):** "Bill's behavior was the reminder to me that coming back to *Star Trek* also meant coming back to meddlesome irritation."

**Norman Spinrad (writer):** "Bill Shatner's problem was that he wasn't given as interesting a character to play as Leonard Nimoy was."

**Nichelle Nichols (Uhura)** (on being interviewed by Shatner for *Star Trek: Memories*): "Aren't you going to ask why we disliked you so much?"

*Buck Rogers in the 25th Century* was one of several sci-fi TV shows that exploded onto our screens in the late 1970s, inspired by the phenomenal success of *Star Wars*. The character had been around since the 1920s, in the form of a newspaper strip, and the basic plot was retained: twentieth-century ace space shuttle pilot is frozen in a freak gas accident, and wakes up 500 years later when everyone wears spandex, but late-twentieth-century haircuts are somehow still in fashion.

Perhaps the most memorable thing about the series (apart from the fact that producer Glen A. Larson recycled props and costumes from his earlier hit *Battlestar Galactica* for the show; and for the second series pretty much recycled the "lost tribes of Israel" plot of *Battlestar Galactica* as well) was Buck's new robot companion, Twiki. If you'd been frozen in time, the last thing you'd want to wake up to is a tiny, tinny buddy who goes "Biddibiddibiddi" all the time—but evidently someone found him endearing.

No less than Mel ("Daffy Duck") Blanc provided his voice for the first series, clearly with a mission to make it as annoying as possible. When not hilariously repeating some twentieth-century saying out of context, Twiki was basically a walking computer station, carrying Dr. Theopolis, the greatest robot mind in the twenty-fifth century. There wasn't much competition. Viewers were reportedly upset when Blanc left, and he was persuaded to return for the final half of the last season.

> **If you could touch the alien sand and hear the cries of strange birds and watch them wheel in another sky, would that satisfy you?**
>
> William Hartnell as the early Dr. Who, on the lure of traveling through time and space

The first really influential science fiction TV series made in Great Britain was *The Quatermass Experiment*, first shown in 1953. For many viewers it was the first time they had seen futuristic elements treated in an adult manner. The series debut was shown shortly after Queen Elizabeth II's coronation, when hundreds of thousands of households had rushed out to buy a newfangled television set, so in effect it was one of the first things this new mass audience was exposed to.

Creator Nigel Kneale spotted the name Quatermass while browsing the London Telephone Directory and made a note, thinking it would be a striking name for a character, and he was right. Professor Bernard Quatermass was a rather upright scientist, initially head of the British Experimental Rocket Group, who finds himself battling to save mankind from strange and sinister aliens, while humanity in general remains oblivious. In the first series, Howard Tate played him, but the actor died before filming could start on *Quatermass II*. John Robinson replaced him for the 1955 sequel, which was another huge hit. However, Robinson didn't feel quite right to either writer or director (Rudolph Cartier), so for the third and final adventure, *Quatermass and the Pit*, he was replaced by André Morell.

1958's *Quatermass and the Pit* introduced the theme of hidden alien legacies in human history to television, which would be taken up again and again by everyone from Erich Von Däniken to Chris Carter. Thames Television made a fourth and final adventure; by 1979, Sir John Mills was tackling the character. And in 2005, a groundbreaking live broadcast, a remake of the original series, was shown on BBC Four.

> **It sounds a little presumptuous, but I think that *Star Trek* provides a mythology for people in a culture that has no mythology.**
>
> William Shatner, who played Captain James Tiberius Kirk in *Star Trek*

## SEXIEST SPACE SIRENS — TV'S TOP FANTASY FEMMES

**Diana Rigg** (Emma Peel, *The Avengers*)

**Jacqueline Pearce** (Servalan, *Blake's 7*)

**Gillian Anderson** (Dana Scully, *The X-Files*)

**Janet Fielding** (Tegan Jovanka, *Doctor Who*)

**Jewel Staite** (Kaylee Frye, *Firefly*)

**Eliza Dushku** (Tru Davies, *Tru Calling*)

**Julie Newmar** (original Catwoman, *Batman*)

**Denise Crosby** (Tasha Yar, *Star Trek*)

**Jessica Alba** (Max Guevera, *Dark Angel*)

**Alyson Hannigan** (Willow, *Buffy the Vampire Slayer*)

**Jeri Ryan** (*Seven of Nine, Star Trek: The Next Generation*)

**Jennifer Garner** (Sydney Bristow, *Alias*)

**Louise Jameson** (Leela, *Doctor Who*)

**Gabrielle Drake** (Lt. Gay Ellis, *UFO*)

**Pamela Hensley** (Princess Ardala, *Buck Rogers*)

**Lady Penelope Crighton-Ward**
(as voiced by Sylvia Anderson, *Thunderbirds*)

**Sarah Michelle Gellar** (Buffy Summers, *Buffy the Vampire Slayer*)

**Yvonne Craig** (Batgirl, *Batman*)

**Wendy Padbury** (Zoe, *Doctor Who*)

**Erin Gray** (Col. Wilma Deering, *Buck Rogers*)

1. *Star Trek* contained the first interracial kiss shown on primetime TV in America. It was in the episode "Plato's Stepchildren," and was between Kirk and Lieutenant Uhura.

2. Leonard Nimoy's character, Mr. Spock, was originally supposed to have red skin and a tail.

3. *Star Trek* created the world's most famous split infinitive with its mission: "To boldly go where no man has gone before." For *Star Trek: The Next Generation*, it was changed to, "Where no one has gone before" to reflect a more P. C. culture, but the split infinitive remained.

4. Captain Kirk romanced his way across the universe, not letting green skin or alien DNA put him off spreading his seed among the stars. Every week he had a new true love. On-screen conquests included Angelique Pettyjohn, Kathie Brown, and Joan Collins.

5. Captain Kirk got to fight himself five times, thanks to *Star Trek* writers, who obviously realized William Shatner's preferred acting partner was himself. In "The Enemy Within" and "Mirror Mirror," he gets split into two beings, good and evil sides of himself. In "What Are Little Girls Made Of?" he's attacked by an android replica of himself. In "Turnabout Intruder," a woman swaps bodies with him, and in the sixth *Star Trek* film, a shapeshifter takes on his image.

Part of the problem is that many reporters have come to expect, and come to associate that SF-shows = crap. Or kids' stuff. They've gotten very jaded with the same old promises every year. So on that level, it's understandable.

Michael J. Straczynski on the press response to *Babylon 5*

Happily for us, English turns out to be the *lingua franca* of the entire universe. That's the only sensible explanation. The only other alternative, used by *Star Trek* and *The Simpsons*, is that English sounds like a lot of other languages. As the tentacled alien Kang in *The Simpsons* put it '"Actually I'm speaking Rigellian. By an astonishing coincidence our two languages are exactly the same!"

### Star Trek

**Bajoran** – only a handful of words exist, including those for ghost and go away!

**Ferengi** – extensively developed by fans, in the shows the Ferengi utterances tend to be along the lines of "Never give a sucker an even break"

**Kardasi** – 29-character language spoken by Cardassians

**Klingon** – the Klingon name for Klingon is tlhIngan Hol, created by linguist Mark Okrand

**Linguacode** – a picture-based language system used in *Star Trek* for first contact with alien races

**Romulan** – sounds like a combination of Latin and Welsh

**Tarmarian** – from *Star Trek: The Next Generation*, the language spoken by The Children of Tama, who communicate only in parables just to make it that bit more complicated

**Vulcan** – very few Vulcans have spoken any Vulcan on screen, but three very different written scripts (one suggesting curvasive Japanese, another Mongolian, and a third block cut geometric symbols) have appeared.

### Star Wars

**Ewokese** – created by mixing Tibetan, Mongolian, and Nepalese

**Wookie** – appears to consist of random moans and groans, but has a name: Shyriiwook

### Others

**Chakobsa** – the secret Fremen language spoken in the *Dune* TV series

**Goa'uld** – from *Stargate-SG1*, the language of an evil symbiotic snake alien that likes to burrow into human brains and take them over, based on Ancient Egyptian

**Tenctonese** – language of the alien slaves on Earth in *Alien Nation*

**Bork-Bork-Bork** – the mock Swedish language spoken by Chef on *The Muppet Show*

Irwin Allen earned the nickname "The Master of Disaster" because he produced so many disaster movies, including *The Poseidon Adventure* and *Towering Inferno*. But he was also producer of many mad 1960s sci-fi adventure shows that revolved around gimmicky plots. But for viewers too young to remember the shows, he's probably just as well-known for being name-checked by thrash group Killdozer in *Man vs. Nature*. His sci-fi career only lasted a few years, and his shows were full of bad effects, plank-like actors, and inconsistent science, but somehow they worked.

*Voyage to the Bottom of the Sea* (1964–68) centered around the Seaview, a kind of underwater *Enterprise*, the world's first privately owned nuclear submarine, wetly going where no vessel had ventured, and discovering that the seabed is full of men in rubber suits pretending to be creatures from the Black Lagoon.

*Lost in Space* (1965–68) was started a year after *Voyage* debuted successfully. Professor Robinson and his family set off (all half-dozen of them) to establish a space colony to relieve the desperately overcrowded planet Earth. Professor Zachary Smith accidentally stows away while trying to reprogram their robot at the behest of an enemy government, and his excess weight means they get lost (honestly!) and spend several series struggling to get back home.

*The Time Tunnel* (1966–67), which overlapped both the above series, begins with "Project Tik-Tok," a government program to create a portal that will allow Americans travel freely in time (you have to ask yourself: why?) It all goes horribly wrong, of course, when two scientists demonstrate it for an impatient senator and wind up on the *Titanic* just before it sinks. They then begin to ricochet around, lost in time, always turning up just as some major historical event is going down, an idea that would be reprised in *Quantum Leap*.

Allen's final show in a flurry of fantasy activity was *Land of the Giants* (1967–70). A spaceship's crew crash-lands on planet Earth where everyone is a giant, living in giant cities, driving giant cars. No explanation is ever given as the tiddly refugees try and stay out of the clutches of giant scientists who want to study them—or sometimes just squish them.

The future never looked more, well, futuristic than in Gerry Anderson's first live sci-fi show, *UFO* (1970), which insisted that in the very near future we'd all be wearing purple wigs and silver mini skirts. (OK, just the women, the men got lamé zip-up suits and bleach jobs). It wasn't as mad as it sounds, as the show was only set in 1980, 10 years in the future, when Earth was being attacked by aliens, and the fashions were really 1960s ones taken to extremes. What was mad is the thought that in a mere decade we'd have managed to develop *Star Wars*-style defense satellites, a MoonBase from which to launch spacecraft, and undersea aircraft launchers.

MoonBase was where all the purple wigs came in. Every woman on the Moon had one—as well as huge false eyelashes, pouty lips, and a trim figure. Gerry Anderson thought glittery things and wigs looked better under harsh studio lights, while his wife, perhaps grasping at straws here, declared she believed wigs would be part of military uniforms by the next decade.

However, in some areas *UFO* got it right on. Among other things, its vision of the future included car telephones, voice identification systems, and Space Shuttle-style launches of one spacecraft from another.

There is nothing wrong with your television set. Do not attempt to adjust the picture. We are controlling transmission. If we wish to make it louder, we will bring up the volume. If we wish to make it softer, we will tune it to a whisper. We can reduce the focus to a soft blur, or sharpen it to crystal clarity. We will control the horizontal. We will control the vertical. For the next hour, sit quietly and we will control all that you see and hear. You are about to experience the awe and mystery which reaches from the inner mind to . . . The Outer Limits!

The spooky voiceover and fuzzy screen always set the tone for this classic TV show

*The Twilight Zone* and *The Outer Limits* thrilled and frightened TV viewers in the 1960s. Although some of the men in rubber suits and puppet monsters may seem laughable now, at the time they mesmerized audiences. One episode of *The Outer Limits* that still has the power to send a chill up your spine is "The Zanti Misfits," first shown on December 30, 1963.

Featuring a young Bruce Dern, the story is about a deal struck by the rulers of the advanced planet Zanti to export their criminals to Earth, because they can't bring themselves to kill them—too evolved, and all that. "Throughout history, compassionate minds have pondered this dark and disturbing question," begins the series' trademark opening narration, always delivered by Vic Perrin. They believe, quite rightly you suspect, that when humans encounter the large insect beings with strangely human heads, they will be terrified and their instinct will be to destroy them.

The Zanti demand total privacy when they arrive on Earth to deliver their "misfits" (presumably so we Earthlings don't run amok in a fit of revulsion and kill them all), but unfortunately two earth criminals accidentally blunder into the restricted area, see the Zanti's secret, and therefore must die.

The episode really trades on most people's fear of scuttling, skittering, chitinous insects crawling all over you, and remains memorable for many sci-fi fans more than 40 years after it was first made.

> I realized that by creating a futuristic world where new rules applied, I could make statements about present day issues such as sex, religion, Vietnam, unions, politics, and intercontinental ballistic missiles.
>
> Gene Roddenberry, creator / producer, *Star Trek*

The original *Star Trek* attracted some well-regarded names from the science fiction community as scriptwriters, including Norman Spinrad ("The Doomsday Machine"), Richard Matheson ("The Enemy Within") and Theodore Sturgeon ("Shore Leave"). But the best regarded episode in the entire run is "The City on the Edge of Forever," first broadcast in April 1967. It was scripted by firebrand sci-fi writer Harlan Ellison, who is legendary in TV circles for punching out an executive who made the mistake of telling him: "You'll write what I tell you to write." In the end several of Ellison's more radical ideas—an *Enterprise* crew member dealing drugs and fleeing through time being the cause of all the trouble, Kirk being unwilling to give up the girl to save the world—didn't make it to the small screen, and the writer wound up putting his sarcastic pen name Cordwainer Bird on the finished product. But what did make it earned the series its one and only Emmy.

The plot has Dr. McCoy accidentally injecting himself with a drug that turns him mad. He transports to a mysterious planet, which contains a gateway to time, and leaps through. Kirk and Spock follow and find they're back in America during the Great Depression. Unknown to them they've arrived before McCoy, and are altering the way history will turn out. It was not the first time they'd done this. In "Tomorrow Is Yesterday," the whole Enterprise accidentally goes back to the 1960s, which causes a chronological snafu.

Unless Kirk allows the ideological, peace-loving social worker he just happens to have fallen in love with to die in an accident, instead of saving her, America won't enter WWII early enough and the Nazis will develop the A-Bomb first, and take over the world. The complicated and emotive storyline survived two rewrites by Ellison and further interference from Roddenberry. (Ellison has since published the three script variants.)

# Legal eagles and medicine men

SOME OF THE LONGEST-RUNNING AND MOST
POPULAR SHOWS IN TV HISTORY

## SPEAK LIKE THE SOPRANOS

HBO's magnificent mobster-on-the-couch saga has proved one of the most quotable series in living memory. If you want to sound like a Soprano, get with the lingo and the attitude, and fugeddabowdit.

**Tony:** "Which businesses have historically been recession proof?"
**Silvio:** "Certain aspects of the entertainment industry and . . . uh, our thing."

**Big Pussy** (having a nightmare): "I'll shove a rutabaga in your mouth, Jimmy! Keep you quiet!"

**Carmela:** "Jackie Jr. took her into the city to see Aïda."
**Tony:** "I eat her?"

**Dr. Melfi:** "Have you ever had a prostate exam?"
**Tony:** "Are you kidding? I don't let anyone wag their finger in my *face*."

**Tony:** "Carmela, there's something I gotta confess . . . What are you doing?"
**Carmela:** "Getting my wine in position to throw in your damn face!"

**Junior:** "You may run North Jersey, but you don't run your Uncle Junior. How many f\*\*king hours did I spend playing catch with you?"

**Big Pussy:** "Not in the face, OK? Give me that? Let me keep my eyes."

## CAREY ON MARIAH

Most irritating appearance by a guest star in *Ally McBeal*? There's a plethora of self-satisfied walk-ons to choose from, but we'd have to plump for the turn telegraphed in by large-chested pop diva Mariah Carey, who showed up in Boston in "Playing With Matches," an episode from the final 2002 season. Carey's blink-and-you'd-miss-it cameo saw her play Candie Cunship (which sounds like the sort of name you'd expect to pop up in a *Carry On* movie), a woman so in love with being in the spotlight that she traveled with her own spotlight and lighting technician to make sure she looked her best at all times. Now that's what you call playing against type.

## SOAP ON A ROPE

It's rare for actors who get their start in hospital soaps to scrabble their way to the top and become bona fide stars—but it can be done.

**John Alderton** – Played dashing Dr. Richard Moon in early British megahit *Emergency-Ward 10*, screened twice weekly by ITV

**Ed Begley, Jr.** – Received six Emmy nominations for his work on NBC's *St. Elsewhere*

**George Clooney** – Was sleeping in a closet in a friend's apartment when he landed the role of hunky Ace in the hospital drama *E/R*. But he didn't become famous until 10 years later, when he became Dr. Douglas Ross on NBC's *ER*—a completely different show

**Richard Chamberlain** – Got his start on *Dr. Kildare*

**Kwame Kwei-Armah** – Played Finlay Newton on popular BBC drama *Casualty*, went on to sing on the BBC's celebrity version of *Pop Idol, Celebrity Fame Academy,* won it and released an album, then morphed into the award-winning playwright of *Elmina's Kitchen*

## ORIGINAL *ER*

You may have wondered, when *ER* first arrived in 1994, why Michael Crichton, who'd written numerous blockbuster novels and screenplays, suddenly wanted to write a medical drama. In fact *ER* was originally planned as a film, and Steven Spielberg was interested in directing. Then Spielberg was introduced to *Jurassic Park*.

The dinosaurs-come-to-life fantasy *Jurassic Park* was much closer in theme to Crichton's early science-fiction books and films (like *Westworld*, set in yet another kind of futuristic amusement park), so *ER* represented a dramatic change of direction for the writer. He had already dealt with medical horror in *Coma*, which he wrote and directed in 1978 from Robin Cook's novel of the same name. Now it was time for a more comforting approach to medical drama. Still, one or two traces of his misspent youth did creep in: Dr. John Carter's name, for instance, comes from the series of books by Tarzan creator Edgar Rice Burroughs, where he was John Carter Warlord of Mars.

Plenty of hit TV shows, from *Ally McBeal* to *The Sopranos*, feature lovingly compiled playlists of mood-inducing songs. *Ally McBeal* is even set in a law practice above a bar, so the characters can pop downstairs for a singsong at will. But the champ for slotting songs in is surely David E. Kelley's previous show, the medical drama *Chicago Hope*. One fan listing documents 140-plus songs in only six seasons, and it's not remotely complete. Obsessives will know that the tunes invariably played during operating sequences, and that the first ancient hit to be exhumed was Gladys Knight's version of "Midnight Train to Georgia," which ran in the pilot show while chief surgeon Jeffrey Geiger wielded the scalpel. Most of the song choices were self-consciously cute:

- Camille drops a donor heart on the floor during transplant surgery. The music is "Chain of Fools."
- Geiger operates on a football player who's had his leg amputated, leaving him unable to earn a living. His theme is "Gimme Some Money."
- Nyland botches an appendectomy. Tom Petty's "You Wreck Me" blares forth.

Still, *Chicago Hope* didn't reveal the full extent of its musical ambitions until a special aired midway through the fourth season. Dr. Aaron Shutt suffers an aneurysm, and experiences weird hallucinations of his colleagues kicking the dust off their heels in a series of all-singing, all-dancing musical extravaganzas. A total of 10 numbers were featured, veering from Dean Martin to Jimi Hendrix, and *Dirty Dancing*'s Kenny Ortega was brought in to choreograph. Of course, the creators hadn't bothered to find out if their stars could sing or dance when they originally cast them, so results were mixed—but all in all, the show was voted a success, and the idea of a musical special was picked up and used again in an acclaimed 2001 episode of *Buffy*. In Buffy's case, the shtick was that the cast got themselves possessed by a music demon from the depths of hell, whose powers left them able to communicate solely via the medium of mainstream West Coast rock.

**If you think back and replay your year, and it doesn't bring you tears of joy or sadness, consider it wasted.**

John Cage, *Ally McBeal*

## STILL WAITING FOR THE VERDICT

Formerly the longest-running legal drama in US TV history, CBS's *Perry Mason* (1957-66) has now been eclipsed by *Law & Order* which, despite changes in cast and several spin offs has been running since 1990. The previous title holder starred Raymond Burr as the eponymous attorney. The original ran for nine seasons and 230 formulaic episodes, and there was a 15-episode revival in 1973—not to mention 10 years' worth of made-for-TV movies, still with the same star. We haven't seen absolutely every episode, but so far as we know, Mason never lost a case in all those years, nor failed to reveal the true murderer in an always-dramatic courtroom twist.

## THE TRIBULATIONS OF DOUGLAS BRACKMAN

*L.A. Law*'s senior partner was there principally as a stooge, injecting comic relief as the lawyer who suffers from every insecurity known to man. Over the years the unfortunate Brackman (played by Alan Richens) . . .

- Got a toupée, which was a source of considerable amusement to everyone who saw it

- Was fitted with braces, and faced the humiliation of another partner telling him he couldn't deal with a client because they wouldn't take a lawyer with braces seriously

- Got treated by a rather dodgy psychiatrist

- Had problems with an awful brother he never knew he had

- Quarrelled dramatically with a neighbor over her noisy dog

- Became a contestant on the game show *Wheel of Fortune* (an episode often considered the point where the show "jumped the shark," as it were)

- Retired to the toilet, lit a cigar and tossed away his lighted match, unaware that someone had dumped turpentine into the bowl

- Discovered his father used prostitutes, slept with his father's favorite gal, then discovered she was actually his mother

Hospitals may be no laughing matter so far as patients are concerned, but doctors have always been renowned for their black humor. A surprising number of shows have tapped into the chucklesome subject of bodily malfunctions and botched operations over the years, including:

### Surgical Spirit
Obscure pitch-black ITV sitcom from the late 1980s—funny, but it had plenty of political points to make. Sharp-tongued Nichola McAuliffe starred.

### Scrubs
Much loved by doctors and nurses, who find it a fairly accurate depiction of hospital humor, this hit US series, which airs on NBC, is played far more for laughs than most of its peers.

### Bodies
Giggle-free BBC3 medical series that's so dark it hardly qualifies as comedy at all. Features a prosthetics workshop that looks like a torture chamber, close-ups of dead babies, and full-frontal cesarean sections.

### Green Wing
Wilfully surreal comedy about the relationships between student doctors and the disturbed (and disturbing) staff at a hospital where there don't seem to be any patients.

### Let the Blood Run Free
Spoof that aired in Australia in the early 1990s. Characters included nurse Pam Sandwich.

### M*A*S*H
Neither as ribald nor as bleak as the famous movie, but struck a chord in American hearts like no other show has done, before or since.

> **People scheduled for surgery may want to avoid this, or they may want to watch in self-defense.**
>
> *New York Times* TV critic Caryn James, on the shenanigans that went on at *Chicago Hope*

# FORBIDDEN (WRINKLED) FRUIT

When it comes to describing the appearance of male leads of a certain age, critics turn to the internationally recognized Klugman Scale, a five-step measure of decrepitude that runs from rumpled, worn, lived-in and sagging through to *Quincy*. But old-timers scoring high marks on the old KS can at least draw comfort from the fact that the eponymous morgue-meister (whose first name was never revealed in the show's seven-year, 147-episode run) led a remarkably active love life for a man nearly ready for his discounted bus pass. Among the numerous girlfriends who "stayed over" on Quincy's houseboat:

• **Lee**, the gorgeous stewardess, who's the doctor's off-and-on girl at the beginning of the run, never minds him cancelling dates at the last moment so he can perform yet another late night autopsy, cooks him meals, does the laundry, and even sands down the deck without a murmur of dissent.

• **Jenny**, an identikit stewardess, who briefly takes Lee's place between the sheets when her predecessor vanishes halfway through the second series without explanation (maybe it's something to do with repetitive stress injury, contracted from too much sanding).

• **Carol**, a rape counselor played by Adrienne Barbeau (who provided the voice for Catwoman in the animated *Batman* TV series).

• **Lynne**, who crops up in series four and gets one of the least believable scenes of the show's entire run. Quincy pops in a few hours after phoning at no notice to cancel yet another date. Instead of throwing her drink over him, she proposes marriage. Although she's a hot blonde "MILF" at least 20 years Quincy's junior, he turns her down. There're just so many more fish in the sea.

• **Laura**, an intern, who helps Quincy out in a particularly worthy episode concerning child abuse. The doc persuades her to hide a battered child, and she agrees, even though she knows she'll lose her dream job if she's caught. "It really doesn't matter," Laura concludes. "I can always go back to work at the department store, selling lingerie and pantyhose." "I'll buy a gross if you're selling them," leers Quincy, ever the perfect gentleman.

• **Dr. Emily Hanover**, the psychologist who becomes the second Mrs. Quincy at the end of the final season, and sings their self-penned wedding vows in an especially saccharine moment. (Anita Gillette, the actress who played Hanover, also appeared in flashbacks as Quincy's deceased first wife.)

• **Nameless Blonde**, the bikini-clad lovely Dr. Q gets to cuddle on the beach at the end of each credits sequence, just to show that 60ish Quincy is indeed one heavy hunk of burning love.

## SIX DEGREES OF SEPARATION

The world of American TV is becoming a very small place, with several shows, like *CSI* and *Law & Order* developing franchises, and others folding into each other.

Begun in 1993, NBC's ***Homicide: Life on the Streets***, in which the characters met their director, Barry Levinson, filming versions of themselves on location . . .

. . . shared plotlines with the early series of

*Law & Order*

. . . which transferred one of its characters (the ever-paranoid John Munch) to . . .

*Law & Order: Special Victims Unit . . .*

*Law & Order* had guest appearances by all but one of the actors who played the attorneys in the first six series of . . .

*The Practice*

. . . which had an episode showing the prosecution's side of a trial where the defense's side was dramatized in creator David E. Kelley's . . .

*Ally McBeal*

. . . and also crossed over with . . .

*Boston Public*

. . . while two of its most popular characters from the last season went on to . . .

***Boston Legal***, which began in 2004.

Odd, isn't it? A country vet sticking his hand up a cow's bottom is acceptable prime-time entertainment. But even the most skilled orthodontists never get a look-in when it comes to commissioning hot medical dramas.

There's no denying that dentists have had a raw deal on TV, in both the US and the UK. Over the years, it seems every other medical speciality imaginable has had its day in the sun: General Practitioners (*Dr. Finlay's Casebook*), vets (*All Creatures Great and Small*), army surgeons (*M\*A\*S\*H*), big-city hospitals (*General Hospital*), airborne doctors (*The Flying Doctors*), Wild West women doctors (*Dr. Quinn, Medicine Woman*), cutting-edge nineteenth-century female surgeons (*Bramwell*), diagnosticians (*House*), forensic pathologists (*CSI*), coroners (*Silent Witness*), and even mature singing detective doctors confronting a plague of murders in their own hospital (*Diagnosis: Murder*, starring, yes, a tap-dancing Dick Van Dyke). But you'd be hard-pressed to find so much as a dental hygienist in a blink-and-you-missed-it guest star role.

Now the *British Dental Journal* has launched a campaign to persuade TV commissioning editors of their profession's appeal: "It's an untapped goldmine waiting to be discovered," *BDJ* editor Mike Grace insists. "We need a hero in a white coat and slightly scuffed white clogs who makes our hearts throb as he reaches for the periodontal probe, unaware he is seconds away from a life-threatening emergency."

You heard the man. Form an orderly line just over there. Oh, and don't forget to floss.

> **Not since *Thirtysomething* has a show divided its viewership so definitively between the camps of "Can't get enough" and "What is this crap?"**
>
> US TV critic Dennis Hensley, commenting on *Ally McBeal*

> **Judge:** "Your motion is denied. I am losing my patience!"
> **Ellenor Frutt:** "To hell with patience, you've lost your *mind*, and that hasn't slowed you down!"
>
> From *The Practice*, a show that was both scathing and cynical when it came to deconstructing the US justice system

## JUDGE NOT, LEST YE BE JUDGED

There must be some sort of clause in the standard network contract offered to the creators of TV law shows: a minimum of one eccentric, absolutely nutty judge per show. No exceptions.

### Ally McBeal
Ally had two total nutjobs on the bench: wattled-up repressed dominatrix "Whipper" Cone, and oral hygiene obsessive "Happy" Boyle ("Show me your teeth!")

### Boston Legal
Judge Clark Brown. "Play the judge!" lawyer Denny Crane advises a colleague. "The man lives with his mother! He wears lifts! The buzz word is nansy-pansy!"

### Hardcastle & McCormick
Judge Milton "Hardcase" Hardcastle recruits a racing-car driver accused of car theft to help him fight crime on the streets. The decrepit judge takes no prisoners and sports T-shirts with slogans

such as, "There's no plea bargaining in heaven."

### Hill Street Blues
Judge Lee Oberman, a rotund, balding character who comes out as a transvestite partway through the show, and takes to wearing dresses and false breasts in court.

### The Simpsons
Judge Snyder, who opens proceedings against Lisa for the destruction of an "angel" she has excavated by chiding her: "Lisa Simpson, you are charged with destruction of an historic curiosity. A misdemeanor. By the larger sum, this trial will settle the age-old question of Science versus Religion. Let the opening statements commence."

The Emmy Award-winning ABC network drama *Boston Legal* features two great characters, Denny Crane and Alan Shore, both arrogant as hell, and both highly entertaining. Crane, played by William Shatner as a pompous womanizer, is matched in self-absorption only by the younger and even more immoral Shore, played with plump smugness by James Spader—who says the things you always wished you'd thought of in moments of crisis.

### Denny Crane's best lines

**Judge:** "Motion for continuance is denied."
"You know what I'm going to do, Brian, just to show you there are no hard feelings? I'm going to sleep with your wife."

"Massachusetts is a Blue State. God has no place here."

"You hear the one about the fella who died, went to the pearly gates? Saint Peter lets him in. Sees a guy in a suit making closing argument. Says, 'Who's that?' Saint Peter says, 'Oh, that's God. Thinks he's Denny Crane.'"

**To Shirley Schmidt (an ex):** "I'm over my wrinkle fetish."

### Alan Shore's best lines

"Hate to extort and run."

**Alan Shore:** "What's your specialty?"
**Psychiatrist:** "Couples counseling. I first saw the client and his wife together. Since the divorce I've been working with him alone."
**Alan Shore:** "So they came to you to improve their relationship, and now one wants to kill the other. Not your best work, was it, doctor?"

**Brad Chase:** "Feel free to make fun of me if you like, but when it comes to making fun of the firm—"
**Alan Shore (interrupting him):** "Let me get this straight, I should feel free to make fun of you . . ."

**Brad Chase:** "I outrank you."
**Alan Shore:** "And I'm such a slut for authority."

On being asked by a judge, when appearing on charges of provoking a brawl at Halloween, why they were consorting with a known prostitute:

**Tara Wilson (dressed as Robin):** "We needed a Catwoman."
**Alan Shore (dressed as Batman):** "With her own whip."

"I'm giving notice, I believe two weeks is standard. Now, step aside before I push you to the ground and go to the toilet on you."

---

**There's no mystery to the appeal of *House*. Within the framework of a formula medical drama, Hugh Laurie has created one of the year's most fascinating new characters, a humorously acerbic, emotionally flawed doctor with little patience for his patients.**

Review in the *Detroit Free Press*, on the latest medical phenomenon, an unlovable American doctor played by English comedian Hugh Laurie, previously best known for portraying arch-idiot Bertie Wooster

## OOGA CHAKA!

*Ally McBeal*'s original USP (Unique Selling Point) was its fantasy sequences, in which the micro-skirted lawyer's hyperactive imagination (and series creator David E. Kelley's use of CGI) subjected her to everything from visions of the famous dancing baby, which symbolized the ever-louder ticking of her biological clock, to being shot through the heart with a whole quiverful of arrows. Although the gimmick was toned down considerably in later series, early episodes featured Ally . . .

- Mutating into a Lolo Ferrari-style monstrosity with gargantuan breasts
- Blowing up Elaine's head until she looks like Betty Boop
- Biting off someone's head, literally
- Growing a gigantic tongue
- Committing an embarrassing faux pas, then inserting her foot into her mouth
- Being hurled into a garbage truck when a former lover tells her: "I don't think you and I are going to work out."
- Donning enormous boxing gloves to pummel love rival Georgia
- Daydreaming about Al Green performing in her firm's unisex bathroom

# Twisted TV

## FROM THE DISTURBINGLY ODD TO THE FRIGHTENINGLY FREAKISH

David Lynch's *Twin Peaks* was the weirdest show ever to make it to network television—disturbing, mind-boggling, and humorous in equal measure.

Number of Golden Globes won by the series: **3**

Number of black suits Agent Cooper owns: **5**, one for each day of the week.

Number of recycled names in the show: **5**. Gerard, the one-armed man is named after the detective seeking Richard Kimble in *The Fugitive*. Agent Gordon Cole is named after a character in *Sunset Boulevard*. Madeleine Ferguson is a combination of the male and female leads in *Vertigo*. And Walter Neff, the insurance agent, takes his name from the crooked insurance agent in *Double Indemnity*.

Number of *Twin Peaks* regulars who went on to portray characters on *Seinfeld*: **6** (Warren Frost, Ian Abercrombie, Frances Bay, Walter Olkewicz, Molly Shannon, Grace Zabriskie). Six, including David Duchovny, went on to appear on *The X-Files*.

Number of shows after which the show was withdrawn from German TV: **20** (a rival network revealed the killer's identity).

Number of years older Agent Cooper is in his dreams of the red room: **25**

Percentage of audience the pilot episode of *Twin Peaks* got: **33**%

Distance at which Agent Cooper's rock breaks a bottle in his mystic Tibetan "find the killer" experiment: **60** feet **6** inches

Original population of Twin Peaks: **5,120** (later changed to 51,200)

## I am not a number, I am a free man!

Patrick McGoohan as Number 6 in *The Prisoner*

> **Television has done much for psychiatry by spreading information about it, as well as contributing to the need for it.**
>
> Alfred Hitchcock

## KEEP IT IN THE FAMILY

Although it may seem that *The Munsters* was a facsimile of *The Addams Family*, both shows actually debuted within a week of each other in September 1964. Neither lasted, but both have become rather strange comedy classics whose distinctive look and macabre humor found new audiences in the 1980s and 1990s, leading to *The Addams Family* being made into two successful films.

*The Addams Family* was based on Charles Addams' series of darkly humorous cartoons from *The New Yorker*. Making something as vulgar as a TV series put an end to his family outings, however, and after the show debuted only occasional single character cartoons appeared in that august publication.

Addams made few contributions to the show, but he did name the characters who, apart from Cousin It, had never had names. Gomez almost

wound up being called Repelli (from repellant), but luckily John Astin preferred Gomez for his character. Another early change was Pugsley, who was originally to be called Pubert; several people thought it sounded too sexual so the name was altered. The other major contribution Addams made to the show was the look of the Addams' home. The producers were inspired by Addams' own New York apartment and ignored the creepy castle look of the original cartoons.

Several other alterations to the original concept were made. Addams originally depicted Uncle Fester as a solitary figure, never with the family. On one occasion he's seen with the children, dynamiting fish, but no cartoons of the adult Addamses together exist except for a family portrait. The TV Fester remained a shy and slightly reclusive figure, however.

Debuting in 1993, *The X-Files* ran for nine successful seasons of conspiracies, alien abductions, and strange goings-on in the woods. Ranked the second-best cult show of all time (behind *Star Trek*) by *TV Guide*, it's not surprising that many shows tried to copy its success.

Creator Chris Carter spun off a series about Mulder's three geeky conspiracy friends, *The Lone Gunmen*, and in the run-up to 2000 created *Millennium*—a show whose worldview was, if possible, even more paranoid and disturbing. *Millennium* briefly crossed over with *The X-Files*, but Carter's third series of the period, 1999's *Harsh Realm*, set within a virtual reality war game, did not.

None of these shows quite captured the popular imagination as *The X-Files* had done, but that didn't stop others having a go. *The Burning Zone*, launched in 1996, was one of the first, centering on the weird missions of a top-secret biological task force. That year we also got *Dark Skies*, based on an alternative history in which aliens have been on Earth since the 1940s.

*Strange World* debuted in 1999, as did *Roswell*—a show in which alien-human hybrid children with super powers hide out on Earth and, er, go to school. 2000's *Mysterious Ways* suggested strange forces influencing events in human life. *Special Unit 2* sought to marry *Buffy* and *The X-Files* by having Chicago cops hunting down monsters. The most recent spawns of *The X-Files* are the most interesting: *Carnivale* is set in the Dust Bowl during the Great Depression, among a troupe of traveling entertainers with strange powers, and *The 4400* is about what happens when a large group of abductees suddenly reappear on Earth.

## I plan on writing an epic poem about this gorgeous pie.

Agent Gordon Cole (played by David Lynch himself), on first tasting *Twin Peaks* cherry pie

## WHAT KILLED KENNY

Every episode the creators of Comedy Central's animated *South Park* tried to come up with a madder, odder, or sicker way to dispose of parka-clad Kenny. He was shot seven times, impaled and drowned twice each and run over by a train, a bus, a sled, a motorcycle, Officer Barbrady's police car, and an ambulance. Our top 10 faves:

1. Gored by a bull
2. Head blown off by a firework
3. Head bitten off by Ozzy Osborne
4. Sucked into a giant fan
5. Crushed by a Russian space station reentering the Earth's atmosphere
6. Defecates himself to death
7. Hit by his own falling gravestone
8. Battered to death by a monster Christina Aguilera with a frying pan
9. Pecked to death by turkeys
10. Dies laughing

## DEAD GOOD

It's quite hard for those who didn't see it and who don't remember the stir it caused in the press to believe that *Dead Head* ever existed. Not to be confused with the syndicated US show for fans of the Grateful Dead, this was a 1986 mini series written by Howard Brenton, the man who caused right wing and Christian groups to get their knickers in a twist with his stage play *The Romans in Britain*. *Dead Head* caused such a fuss that Brenton didn't write another TV script until 2002, when he contributed several episodes to the first series of *Spooks* (known in the US as *MI-5*).

Denis Lawson headed a critically acclaimed cast—which included Simon Callow, Lindsay Duncan, Don Henderson, and George Baker—playing a petty thief who gets involved in the shadowy, amoral world of espionage and winds up carrying around a severed head in a bag. Very grim and very violent, it paved the way for a new wave of gritty TV dramas, much as *The Sweeney* did in the 1970s.

classic tv

# CRAZY PLOTS FROM *SAPPHIRE & STEEL* (1978)

All the six storylines featuring the time-fighting duo (Joanna Lumley as Sapphire, David McCallum as Steel) are pretty incomprehensible, so we have to include them all. Despite careful viewings, we have to admit that not a great deal makes sense . . . but that's all part of the series' charm.

### Escape Through the Cracks of Time

The parents of two children, living in a remote house, disappear just as S&S materialize and are menaced by some Roundheads and plague victims. Eventually the agents lure the unnamed menace to the house's cellar, and an agent called Lead helps them crush it through the floor.

### The Railway Station

A force called The Darkness is feeding on the resentment of people who've died prematurely at a railway station. It takes over Sapphire and she attacks Steel with a bunch of flowers, but eventually Steel bargains with the force to put time right. Giving away time makes Time resentful, and The Darkness feeds off this resentment. We think.

### The Creatures' Revenge

Visitors from the future are doing an experiment living on top of a block of flats and are menaced by Time, which is jealous because all animals are extinct in their future. It plies their baby with animal products and gives it power to age things.

### The Man Without a Face

In a junk shop being run by a faceless timeshifter called Shape, Sapphire and Steel discover the old landlord's tenant stuck in a photo. The menace burns her and traps S&S, but they're rescued by a heroic stripper, trick Shape into a kaleidoscope, and put it on a sinking ship.

### Dr. McDee Must Die

During an anniversary party, time moves back 50 years and the guests start being killed off. S&S realize the events leading to the death of scientist Dr. McDee are being recreated, in the hope that instead of being destroyed the lethal virus he has invented will be unleashed and devastate humanity.

### The Trap

S&S arrive at a highway rest stop, and people from different eras start to appear. The agents are suspicious due to an unused tambourine and their companions' lack of interest in modern technology. Eventually they realize they're Transient Beings, who trap our heroes in the services for all eternity.

Like *The X-Files*, *Twin Peaks* was a unique and arresting show that sucked in its viewers with a labyrinthine plot with layer after layer of revelations. Unlike *The X-Files*, the series wasn't a massive success, but it did influence a lot of shows that came after it. The first person to be inspired by it was Oliver Stone, who produced a perplexing mini-series in 1993, with episodes directed by the likes of Keith Gordon and Kathryn Bigelow. *Wild Palms* took a hard look at corporate America, media control and religious manipulation. A few communities try to resist the "march of progress," but the show portrays an America brainwashed by television. The approach to plotting and characterization is very close to Lynch's work, and among Stone's finest.

Two years later, borrowing heavily from the menacing atmosphere of *Twin Peaks*, came *American Gothic*, a mix of horror story and thriller, set in the small South Carolina town of Trinity, where dark forces seem to be at work. The story is driven by the love / hate relationship between the local sheriff Lucas Buck, who seems to be at the center of all the death

and destruction, and his son, Caleb Temple, who didn't know Buck was his father for many years. When Buck suddenly takes an interest in the horrified Caleb, several forces gather to try and save the boy from his inheritance.

Two shows from the period which took *Twin Peaks*' quirkiness without its more disturbing side are *Due South*, about a Canadian mountie and his pet wolf whose old-fashioned manners are out of step with the big city he's sent to work in; and *Northern Exposure*, which follows a yuppie doctor to his posting in a strange but benevolent Alaskan outpost.

Still, in small-town territory there's also *Wolf Lake* (2001), which was cancelled after one season, despite campaigns to save it by its ardent fans. Set in a small backwoods town where humans and werewolves have held an uneasy truce for decades, things begin to fall apart when a power struggle among the local werewolf clans coincides with the arrival of John Kanin, a detective (played by Lou Diamond Phillips) looking into the disappearance of his girlfriend.

Every episode of *Six Feet Under*, which aired on HBO for four seasons, opened with a sudden death, which would be followed through that episode. Over the seasons the writers came up with more and more bizarre and ironic ways to go including:

**Jesse Ray Johnson** – motorbike accident while (dressed as Santa Claus) waving to some kids

**Chloe Anne Bryant Yorkin** – sticks her head out of a car sunroof to shout "I'm the king of the world," and gets her skull smashed

**Lawrence Henry Mason** – is struck by lightning after stealing an umbrella

**Kaitlin Elise Stolte** – dies laughing at a prank call made by two of her girlfriends

**Thomas Alfredo Romano** – mangled in an industrial dough mixer

**Lawrence Tuttle** – crushed beneath his comic book collection

**Anahid Hovanessian** – hit by blue ice (frozen urine) that falls off a plane while she's in her garden trying to get a mobile phone signal

**Jean Louise McArthur** (aka porn star Viveca St. John) – accidentally electrocuted when her cat jumps into the bath

**Samuel Wayne Hoviak** – run over by his own car (he leaves the engine running while going to pick up a newspaper from his driveway)

**Matthew Heath Collins** – falls off a boat drunk and is minced by its propeller

---

**Violence and smut are of course everywhere on the airwaves. You cannot turn on your television without seeing them, although sometimes you have to hunt around.**

Author Dave Barry

---

Deciding who's good and who's bad is one of the great pleasures of the ABC castaway hit *Lost*:

**Dr. Jack Sheppard (Matthew Fox)**
**Good:** Saintly rescuer of passengers from the plane wreckage. Leader and all-American hero. Handily a world-renowned surgeon, too.
**Evil:** Shopped his drunken surgeon father, helped Sayid torture Sawyer, appeared to abandon kidnapped Claire after one warning from Ethan.

**Sayid Jarrah (Naveen Andrews)**
**Good:** Engineers Nadia's escape; feels very guilty for past acts.
**Evil:** Republican Guard torturer who used sharpened palm fronds on Sawyer with some relish.

**Claire Littleton (Emilie de Ravin)**
**Good:** At first, seems the epitome of sunny wholesomeness.
**Evil:** Prepared to give away her baby for adoption. By episode six we're wondering if she's bearing the Antichrist.

**John Locke (Terry O'Quinn)**
**Good:** Regional collector for a box company who's good at "providing for" camp.
**Evil:** Weird retina changes to black and white, fondness for skinning and gutting boar, only paraplegic to travel with a case full of knives.

**Kate Austin (Evangeline Lilly)**
**Good:** Beautiful, hardy, brave, and always happy to volunteer for a search or to kiss Sawyer.
**Evil:** Pathological liar, bank robber who double-crossed and shot accomplices.

**Charlie Pace (Dominic Monaghan)**
**Good:** His name means "Peace" but this former choirboy failed to find any in a rock band. Rescued Jack from cave-in.
**Evil:** Caused the rock fall that he saved Jack from. Hopeless junkie barely holding drug renunciation together.

**"Hurley" Reyes (Jorge Garcia)**
**Good:** The big friendly guy most likely to say "What up?" Built golf course over concerns everyone was too stressed.
**Evil:** "I used to be considered something of a warrior myself back home." This does not bode well.

**Jin Kwom (Daniel Dae Kim)**
**Good:** Humble man who loved the boss's daughter, Sun Kwom, and wooed and married her.
**Evil:** Apparently involved in killing the boss's enemies to close the deal,

which suited his increasingly vicious temperament—insanely jealous.

**Sun Kwom (Yoon-jin Kim)**
**Good:** Happy with a gift of a single flower in the first days of her courtship. Helped Shannon survive with herbal medicine.
**Evil:** Sly minx who learned English while planning to flee her husband and pretend to be dead.

**Michael Dawson**
**(Harold Perrineau, Jr.)**
**Good:** Protective of son Walt Lloyd. A builder by trade, he rigs up showers in the caves.
**Evil:** Immediately accused Jin of racism. Refused to allow Walt to befriend the Jins or Locke.

**"Sawyer" Ford (Josh Holloway)**
**Good:** Couldn't bring himself to ruin another child's life just because his had been ruined by a conman.
**Evil:** Despite life being ruined by a conman, becomes one himself. Withholds asthma medication even under torture, then reveals he never had it anyway.

## PUTTING THE "MRS." IN MRS. PEEL

Nowadays we don't tend to give it much thought, but when *Avengers* character Emma Peel, played by Diana Rigg, was introduced, the show's producers were at pains to make it clear she was a married woman . . . albeit a widowed one. The premise was that Mrs. Peel—as she was frequently referred to—was the widow of Peter Peel, a pilot who'd crashed in mysterious circumstances, and was still faithful to his memory despite her verbal sparring with Steed.

This allowed the writers to create not so much a "Will they, won't they?" as a "Do they, don't they?" scenario between the two. Rigg and Patrick MacNee as Steed shared a crackling on-screen chemistry and while some fans maintain they kept a respectful distance, others interpreted it to mean that they were quietly having sex off camera—perhaps a touch of wish-fulfillment going on?

Mrs. Peel is written out of the series when her husband, Peter, suddenly reappears in "The Forget-Me-Not" (1968). You never see Peter's face, but from the back he looks identical to Steed, even down to the trademark headgear. Having given Steed a quick kiss she advises her replacement, Tara King (played plank-like by Linda Thorson) to remember to stir Steed's tea counterclockwise, and is gone, leaving thousands of men dreaming of her tight-fitting cat suits and karate kicks.

# Housewives' choice

## choice

SELF-HELP, DOMESTIC HELP AND CELEBRITY
GOSSIP—THE ABSORBING WORLD OF
AFTERNOON TV

When *The Price Is Right* aired on Saturdays in the UK in 1984, it was a revelation. Fast and brash and distinctly American, the show grabbed a huge audience share and became something of a cult among youngsters who'd never normally admit to liking a quiz show. Hosted by Leslie Crowther, British viewers had never seen an audience whipped up into such a frenzy, and in Thatcherite Britain it seemed like a hymn to consumerism—based, as it was, around guessing the current retail price of row after row of groceries, electronic and household goods, cars and holidays.

America had been enjoying the *Price Is Right* phenomenon since 1972, when the modern version began broadcasting as a daytime show with Bob Barker at the helm. Since then Barker has missed taping only three episodes. Earlier, in 1956, Bill Cullen had hosted a rather more restrained version (although they did give away a live elephant in one show, which predictably decided to go to the bathroom as soon as the camera was turned on it). After over 6,000 shows, phrases like "Come on down!" have entered popular parlance, and versions of *The Price Is Right* have been made as far afield as Indonesia and Finland. Little has changed over the years. The show has kept the same theme song and the same games—and this, the producers and host believe, is the secret of its success, making it the longest-running game show in America, and probably the world.

> **You can't watch it without being convinced that the Americans are doomed, and this is a comforting feeling for many, despite the fact that all of the most sophisticated TV comedy is American. Springer assembles the white trash, not to mention the black trash, the Hispanic trash, and every other category of bozo in these United States, and sets them loose to abuse one another for our entertainment.**
>
> TV critic Declan Lynch writing in *The Irish Independent*

People get pretty worked up on daytime talk shows. And the producers of the shows don't exactly encourage them to stay calm and collected—after all, if everyone sat around calmly and discussed the issue in a mature and sensible way we'd have *After Dark*, not Jerry Springer. Threats, fisticuffs, "Talk to the hand, cause the head ain't listening" and storming off are all part of the daily talk show diet.

Yet despite their fondness for histrionics, few TV producers thought their shows could do any harm . . . until Jonathan Schmitz shot and killed his neighbor, Scott Amedure, after Amedure had ambushed him on an episode of *Jenny Jones* ("Same Sex Secret Crushes") and told Schmitz he was infatuated with him. Schmitz was sentenced to 25–50 years in prison in 1999, and the show on which he appeared was never broadcast, although strangely, permission to air clips was granted to other TV shows. Amedure's family sued the producers and succeeded in getting a court to award them $25 million, saying Schmitz had a record of substance abuse, mental illness, depression, and was known to be homophobic, but the verdict was overturned at appeal. Schmitz claimed the show had led him to believe his secret admirer was a woman, although Jenny Jones repeatedly stated that he knew in advance he might be confronted by a man. However in court she admitted, "I cared that he not know [that the person who had a crush on him was a man], otherwise we wouldn't have had a show."

The *Jerry Springer* show was also implicated in a murder in July 2000, when shortly after finishing taping "Secret Mistresses Confronted," one of the guests was found dead in Florida. Her former husband was arrested for the murder.

> **Thank God we're living in a country where the sky's the limit, the stores are open late, and you can shop in bed thanks to television.**
> Joan Rivers, who should be in favor of shopping channels, given that she flogs her own line of jewelry on QVC.

# BEST JERRY SPRINGER SHOW TITLES

The problem with Jerry is there's just so much to choose from. Dwarves, one-legged thieves, sadomasochists, and men in diapers, the Ku Klux Klan and baked bean wrestlers . . . where do you start?

1. "I Married a Horse!"
2. "My Husband Had Sex with My Brother"
3. "Pregnant By a Transexual"
4. "I'm a Breeder for the Klan"
5. "I Gave Myself an Abortion"
6. "My Teen Worships Satan!"
7. "I Cut Off My Manhood!"
8. "My Parrot Runs My Life!"
9. "You're Too Fat to Make Porn"
10. "I'm on Springer . . . and I'm Mad"

## QUEENS OF THE TALK SHOW

### US: Oprah Winfrey

When it comes to daytime talk shows, Oprah is the queen, empress, grand poobah of them all. Broadcasting from Harpo Studios (which she owns; the name is Oprah backward) in Chicago (large chunks of which she also probably owns), Oprah is a true talk-show phenomenon. A personal recommendation on her show creates box-office records and bestsellers, and by sharing her difficult past repeatedly with viewers, she manages to be a multimillionaire, yet somehow seem to be a "normal," down-to-earth person, just like any of her audience.

### UK: Trisha Goddard

Conceived as the UK's answer to Oprah, *Trisha* (later retitled *Trisha Goddard* when the show switched to Channel 5) is made in East Anglia, and its host became increasingly Ricki / Springeresque in her approach to themes, with shock revelations, paternity, and lie detector tests and sexual hijinks highlighted. Trisha trades on her hard life as a single mother, and has a very firm, candid style when she dislikes guests.

For those who prefer to avoid the gym, television has proved to be a surrogate fitness teacher, with shows in the 1950s teaching us to swing clubs in a healthful fashion, and the 1960s encouraging us to make like a human pretzel watching yoga. By the 1980s, TV fitness instructors had become celebrities in their own right. Here are our favorites:

### Mr. Motivator – Derrick Errol Evans

Bespectacled, ultra-friendly Jamaican guy who, you suspect, would give you a big hug the first time he met you. A favorite of UK morning TV, he now runs fitness events at Center Parcs and owns H'Evans Scent, a Jamaican retreat.

### Mad Lizzie – Lizzie Webb

Also a hugger, but in a much more demented fashion. Lizzie was TV-am's first fitness star in the early 1980s. Her trademark was big 80s hair and a succession of garish sweatshirts.

### Green Goddess – Diane Moran

*BBC Breakfast Time*, as befits their mature image, treated us to a few minutes of stretching and jumping with the lycra-clad Green Goddess.

### Denise Austin

In the United States, you're allowed to do TV fitness without having a superhero-style nickname. Austin has been working out on her daily program for 18 years and still looks eerily youthful—there's a portrait somewhere!

### Harvey Walden

Walden, who's still apparently First Sergeant in the US Marines, dispenses training advice on *Celebrity Fit Club* on both sides of the Atlantic. Obviously chosen for his dour mug, his straight talking has gained him a lot of fans. He appears as though his face would crack and fall off if he dared to smile.

### Donna Richardson Joyner, Sweating in the Spirit

Lardy Christians have their own special guru, whose *Sweating In The Spirit* show on The Word Network (America's premiere urban Christian channel) is hugely popular. Six mornings a week she also dispenses advice on mind, body, and spirit.

Considering that it ran for seven years, *Sex and the City* resisted using a lot of celebrity cameos to spice things up, although when it seemed appropriate for the characters to bump into celebs, they would appear, often playing themselves. Here are some recognizable faces to look out for on HBO reruns or on the DVDs:

Candice Bergen – Enid Mead, "A Vogue Idea"

Jon Bon Jovi – Seth, "Games People Play"

Carole Bouquet – Juliette, "American Girl in Paris; Part Deux"

Alan Cumming – O, "The Real Me"

David Duchovny – Jeremy, "Boy, Interrupted"

Carrie Fisher – Herself, "Sex and Another City"

Sarah Michelle Gellar – Debbie, "Escape from New York"

Heather Graham – Herself, "Critical Condition"

Geri Halliwell – Phoebe, "Boy, Interrupted"

Hugh Hefner – Himself, "Sex and Another City"

Heidi Klum – Herself, "The Real Me"

Former New York City mayor Ed Koch – Himself, "The Real Me"

Lucy Liu – Herself, "Coulda, Woulda, Shoulda"

Alanis Morissette – Dawn, "Boy, Girl, Boy, Girl . . ."

Tatum O'Neal – Kyra, "A Woman's Right to Shoes"

Donald Trump – Himself, "The Man, the Myth, the Viagra"

QVC first broadcast to the American public at 7:30 EST on November 24, 1986. The two hosts, Kathy Levine and Bob Bowersox, offered as their very first bargain a shower radio costing $11.49. History doesn't record how many they sold, but it was probably plenty—in its first year of trading, QVC set a record for first year turnover by a public company ($112 million).

One of the channel's most famous products is a trademark fake gemstone called Diamonique, which was scathingly parodied by UK comedy duo French and Saunders. Having bought out MSB Industries, Inc. in 1988, QVC is the only retailer to offer it. Other unique lines include Models Prefer Color, an exclusive makeup range.

QVC's first UK broadcast was on October 1, 1993, in association with BskyB, a UK TV channel bought out by QVC in 2004. To get rid of excess inventory, QVC has two British outlet stores, in Shrewsbury and Warrington.

QVC had its most lucrative trading day on December 4, 2004, although in the run up to Christmas 2005, that record may well be beaten. In 2004, QVC US boasted a net revenue of $4.1 billion.

As well as channels in America and the UK, there are networks in Germany and Japan. All the networks broadcast live 24 hours a day, except for Britain, which can only manage 16 hours of live broadcasts.

Many celebrities have plugged their wares on QVC, including Joan Rivers (jewelry), Britt Ekland (jewelry) and Uri Geller (rock crystal jewelry—Geller's website claims he was a pupil of Dali, and he reportedly sells his drawings on Ebay).

> **I grew up in the world of bad television, on my dad's sets and then as a young schmuck on dating shows and so on.**
>
> George Clooney

## TALK LIKE A WINNER

Jack LaLanne is known as the "father of fitness" to Americans. Now 92, he still appears on TV on both sides of the Atlantic (largely trying to flog his fruit and vegetable juicers). He designed weight machines and invented the jumping jack – and he always had a pithy catchphrase to motivate people:

"People don't die of old age, they die of neglect."

**"No pain . . . No gain . . . take it from LaLanne!"**

"Better to wear out than rust out."

**"Put your muscle where your mouth is."**

"Anything in life is possible if you make it happen."

**"First we inspire them, then we perspire them."**

"I cannot afford to die, it will ruin my image."

## DATING GAMES

The original dating quiz format was conceived by Chuck "Gong Show" Barris in 1965—known in the UK as *Blind Date*. It was the first time people's personal lives had been mixed up with a televised contest, and it proved a huge hit, running until 1986. It attracted extroverts willing to show off their prowess, and was the first taste of TV exposure for early contestants Tom Selleck and Jim Carrey.

Barris also came up with *The Gong Show*—a talent contest where the (often awful) contestants could be "gonged" off when the judges got fed up with their turn—and *The Newlyweds Game* around the same time. The latter format that was again exported to the UK, this time as *Mr. And Mrs.* The British version was very low-key, presented by smooth-talking hosts with a theme tune urging people to "be nice to each other," but the US version was much more risqué, and rumored to have led to some contestants divorcing. The host, Bob Eubanks, would often try to get people to say something with a double meaning, but even he was caught out when he asked a wife what she thought her husband had said to the question "Where is the strangest place you've ever had the urge to make whoopee?" Her answer, "In the butt," was hastily bleeped and Eubanks cracked up. Eventually he managed: "We are looking for a *location*, a *location*."

Back in the 1950s, American TV audiences were outraged to learn that some of the contestants on their most popular quiz shows were getting help with the questions—and plenty of it. This might range from making sure the favored contestant got a topic they were knowledgeable about, to actually giving them the answers. Some directors coached their "members of the public" on how to react well on camera—audiences liked someone who looked eager and like they were thinking hard rather than someone who gave a casual, even arrogant-sounding response. Many of the early quiz shows were sponsored by products, and as such were designed as perfect showcases for that product's brand image. Sponsors also often demanded that they be dramatic, and feature likable winners.

This was the background that led to the scandal that engulfed the hit show *Twenty One* in 1958, events which Robert Redford made into a 1994 film called *Quiz Show* starring the young Ralph Fiennes. Jewish ex-soldier Herb Stempel, who came from a modest background, had been winning for several weeks, thanks in part to hidden helpers. When the sponsors decided it was time for him to go they replaced him with rich, white, intellectual Charles Van Doren, whom they also began to coach and supply with answers. Stempel eventually blew the whistle. As a result, a federal law was drawn up in America prohibiting any kind of fixing on quiz shows. Most networks stopped having individual sponsors for shows, and ratings for all forms of quiz show plummeted rapidly.

The integrity of UK quiz shows remained unchallenged for many more years, until a former army Major, his wife and an intellectual friend came up with what they thought was the perfect scam to trick the producers of the British version of *Who Wants to Be a Millionaire*, hosted by Chris Tarrant. While Major Charles Ingham sat in the hot seat rambling and changing his mind several times before giving a final answer, his wife Diana and superbly-named friend Tecwen Whittock sat in the audience, coughing when he mentioned the correct option to guide his answers. Tarrant admitted afterward that with all the noise going on in the studio he had no idea that they were cheating, and that at the end of taping he called Ingham "an amazing human being." All three were found guilty of conspiracy to cheat the program out of £1 million in April 2003. Ingham has since gone on to become a Z-list celebrity.

# AS INTERESTING AS WATCHING PAINT DRY

TV shows teach us to cook, to clean, to dress well, to put up shelves . . . so why not how to paint? If you're looking for something, shall we say relaxing, look no further than the arty corner of the daytime schedule.

Bob Ross (1942–1995) was the daddy of art show hosts. With his gentle voice and trademark afro, he urged everyone to pick up a brush and try on *Joy of Painting*, believing anyone could paint a landscape if they followed his instructions. For two decades, until his death, amateur artists on both sides of the pond enjoyed Ross's positive attitude—any mistakes were just "happy accidents," and he frequently brought wild animals he'd rescued onto his show.

The UK's answer to Happy Bob was Nancy Kominsky, an American artist who encouraged us to *Paint Along with Nancy* on quiet afternoons in the 1970s. Unlike Bob, Nancy was a towering and rather formidable woman who seemed to work chiefly with a palette knife and roll of toilet paper to correct mistakes. Her British sidekick, Alan Taylor, was there to ask all the questions the viewers might want answered, but he rarely seemed brave enough.

In 1998, Channel 4 had a surprise hit with the daytime painting game show, *Watercolor Challenge*. Hosted by the extremely kind Hannah Gordon, an expert offered tips to two amateurs whose work was judged at the end of the show, and awarded a not very generous prize of artists' materials.

> I still do politics but I do it behind the scenes now. So that's still my passion. It's what I believe most strongly in, and I love that. Do I miss being in elective politics? Sometimes. This show is fun to do, my American show, and it's obviously silly, sometimes stupid. It gives me a good living and I enjoy it but I'm not passionate about it like I am about politics.
>
> Former Mayor of Cincinnati, talk show host Jerry Springer

# Tearjerkers

## THE HELL THAT IS THE
## GROAN-INDUCING TEARJERKER

# GRIZZLY FRIENDS

Living as an outcast in the wilderness, at one with man and beast, you don't form many close friendships. Which kept the supporting cast bill for *The Life and Times of Grizzly Adams* (1977) nice and low. Based on a maudlin 1974 adventure film, the NBC series gave Adams a small but select group of friends who help him aid the few other humans who do stray across his path, all without harming animals, of course, since his best friend is a bear. Those sidekicks in full:

1. **Ben the bear** – adopted as a cub by Adams, the role was played by Bozo the bear. For some reason Ben is a popular name for bears, as there's also *Gentle Ben*, a series about a boy who raises a bear cub

2. **Nakoma the American Indian** – played by Don Shanks

3. **Mad Jack the Mountain Man** – played by Denver Pyle

4. **Number 7 the mule** – Mad Jack's comedy beast of burden, performer's name unknown

# THE LITTLEST HOBO

*The Littlest Hobo* was actually a pretty sizable German shepherd, given a different name by each of the various people who adopt him on his travels. Of course, once his mission is done and his owners' lives are sorted out, the dog is off again. Hobo's adventures ranged from the traditional (rescuing young boy who's adopted him when injured) to foiling spy rings and teaching people the usual moral lessons about being good and caring for each other.

Two series were made, both by Canadian TV: the first in 1963–1965 and the second in 1979–1985. Bizarrely, the dogs used for both series were called London (maybe the producers had trouble remembering names?). The first *Littlest Hobo* series featured a scene that many people remember—perhaps because it was also used in the credit sequence—showing the dog skydiving. What people usually remember from the second series is the theme song: "There's a voice / That keeps on calling me / down the road / Is where I'll always be . . ."

We don't like to speak ill of the dead, but we're going to have to make an exception in this case: Michael Landon was an actor who epitomized the nauseating niceness of family viewing. He starred in not one, but two landmark tearjerkers (*Little House on the Prairie* and *Highway to Heaven*) and died at the height of his career, which is just the perfect icing on a sickly sweet cake for sentimental viewers.

Landon, born Eugene Maurice Orowitz, chose his stage name by flipping through the Los Angeles telephone book until he found one that sounded worthy of an actor. His lucky break came when he landed the lead role in *I Was a Teenage Werewolf* (1957), which led to the role of the youngest Cartwright brother, Little Joe, in *Bonanza*. Landon stayed with *Bonanza* for its entire 14-year run, directing some episodes as well.

The year after *Bonanza*'s cancellation, in 1974, the actor began work on a TV movie based on Laura Ingalls Wilder's charming stories of a frontier family, *Little House on the Prairie*. Not only did he star as the father of the family, the wise and hard-working Charles Ingalls, he also wrote and directed several episodes, and was producer and executive producer of the show. *Little House* was moral with a capital M, and Landon's character was an unassailable paragon of Christian virtue.

You might wonder how Landon could possibly improve on the moral message of his shows. The answer, of course, was by playing an angel. In 1984, he returned to network TV as Jonathan Smith in *Highway to Heaven*. This NBC series followed the generic structure of an intervening force arriving and turning around the troubled lives of deserving people, except this time we had the celestial host instead of a mutt. When Victor French, Landon's co-star on the show, died of lung cancer in 1989, he stopped filming, long before audiences had tired of it.

A couple of years later—having been ditched by NBC despite making three successful series for them—Landon starred in a pilot of a new series, *Us*, but before any further episodes could be filmed, he was diagnosed with pancreatic cancer, which killed him a few weeks later on 1 July 1991.

> Somebody ought to tell us, right at the start of our lives, that we are dying. Then we might live life to the limit every minute of every day. Do it, I say—whatever you want to do, do it now.
>
> The angelic Michael Landon, star of NBC's *Highway to Heaven*

## SKIPPY THE BUSH KANGAROO

"Skippy, Skippy, Skippy the bush kangaroo / Skippy, Skippy, Skippy, your friend ever true." Not the most profound of theme songs, but one that sticks in the memory as does the absurdity of one of the great childhood TV memories from down under. Although it only ran for three years, there were 90 episodes of Skippy (Australia's hopping answer to Lassie) featuring a clever kangaroo that alerted the Hammond children to various mishaps (including smugglers, escaped convicts and people trapped down holes) in the Waratah National Park, where their dad was Head Ranger. The show was a great advertisement for the beauty of the Australian countryside, and featured a lot of shots of Skippy bouncing around.

Skippy was an Eastern Grey kangaroo, played by at least three different animal actors. For a long time it was incorrectly rumored that no one regular kangaroo was featured in the show because, like sheep, no one could tell them apart. Also false is the popular urban legend that after the show finished Skippy got the chop and was turned into dog food.

> I really liked Lassie, but that horse, Flicka, was a nasty animal with a terrible disposition. All the Flickas—all six of them—were awful.
>
> Roddy McDowall on some of his former childhood co-stars

Over the years there have been countless shows, mostly comedies and schmaltzy adventures, featuring helpful animal friends. Along with Black Beauty and Lassie were:

My Friend Flicka – heroic western horse

Mister Ed – hugely popular talking horse
who commented wryly on the action

Champion – The Wonder Horse, friend to orphans

Fury – another wild horse hero, another friend to orphans

Lancelot Link, Secret Chimp – agent of A.P.E., voiced by Dayton Allen

Bear – confusingly, Bear was a monkey (in *B. J. and the Bear*), an idea borrowed straight from Clint Eastwood's 1978 film *Every Which Way But Loose*

Buttons – chimp befriended by a dentist and
his family in *Me and the Chimp*

Gentle Ben – orphaned bear in the series of the same name

Benji – shaggy dog, star of many sentimental shows—including the bizarre sci-fi adventure series *Benji, Zax, and the Alien Prince*

Boomer – the ever-dutiful, elusive mongrel –
"Like magic he appears / A hero to save the day / Just when you think he's here for good / That's when he goes away"

Joe – a military dog pursued after going AWOL to find his old handler (the canine version of *The Fugitive*) in *Run, Joe, Run!*

Cleo – smart basset hound (voiced by Mary Jane Croft) who offers her owner plenty of advice in *The People's Choice*

Arnold – talking pig in the Eddie Albert / Zsa Zsa Gabor
comedy *Green Acres*

Wilder based her books on her memories of childhood in the Midwest in the late-nineteenth century. Weirdly she wrote in the third person, talking about "Laura Ingalls" as though she were a character, and the books are generally classified as fiction by libraries, rather than autobiography.

*Little House in the Big Woods* (1932)
*Little House on the Prairie* (1935)
*On the Banks of Plum Creek* (1937)
*By the Shores of Silver Lake* (1939)
*The Long Winter* (1940)
*Little Town on the Prairie* (1941)
*These Happy Golden Years* (1943)
*The First Four Years* (1971)
*Farmer Boy* (1933) – not, strictly speaking, a *Little House* book,
as it is based on her husband's childhood on a farm in New York State

Six years in grade school, five years in high school—everything I ever ran for, I was always running against the same Johnny Walton . . . The greatest day of my life was when I beat John Walton out for senior class president. I don't think he ever lost any sleep over it. Now I'm an ambitious man—some would say successful; probably it's all John's fault. I was always running; he was always going past me at a walk. And here it is, 25 years later—here I am, and there's John. Then look at me . . . and some of you . . . still running, still wearing ourselves to a frazzle for all sorts of things that John Walton has accumulated while he was out walking—a happy home, a fine wife, and children.

Stanley Grover, who played Bill Shyder from *The Waltons* season seven episode, "The Attack"

Dr. Quinn was certainly a woman ahead of her time, taking the Wild West by storm in CBS's *Dr. Quinn, Medicine Woman* (1993-1998), after being accidentally hired by a small town whose residents obviously think her name (Michaela) is just a slip of the pen, and expect a man instead. Despite plenty of hostility from the townsfolk, in the first season she managed to treat an awful lot of ailments. In the pilot alone, she rattles through lumbago, "women's problems", deafness, childbirth, a rattlesnake bite, a gunshot wound, a broken leg, and a heart attack. Here are the rest of the medical dilemmas she faced in season one:

- Alcohol poisoning
- Anemia
- Asthma
- Bear attack
- Brain hemorrhage
- Blood poisoning
- Broken arm
- Broken wrist
- Burns
- Burst appendix
- Child who's swallowed coins
- Consumption
- Cuts and gashes
- Diabetes
- Dislocated shoulder
- Drowning
- Fever
- Flu — an epidemic sweeps through the town in pre-antibiotic days
- Frostbite
- Gunshot wounds (lots)
- Head injuries
- Heart attacks
- Hernia
- Mercury poisoning — another epidemic, it gets into the water supply
- Ovarian cyst
- Paralysis
- Trichinosis

---

**If you don't want to be pitied for being a cripple in a wheelchair, don't come out of the house.**

Jerry Lewis, America's Labor Day Telethon king, takes a rather insensitive view of disability in a May 20, 2001 interview on *CBS News Sunday Morning*. He was responding to criticisms about hosting America's longest-running telethon and other remarks he'd made about the "differently abled"

Living up a mountain during the Great Depression (and nine out of ten historians would probably agree with us here) was surely less fun and less rewarding than *The Waltons* made it seem. Ma and Pa may not always have had shoes, but they certainly found time to have a whole slew of kids. As the gloomy pop singer Morrissey put it: "A double bed, and a stalwart lover for sure / These are the riches of the poor."

*The Waltons* ran from 1972 to 1981, and several film-length specials followed to keep fans up-to-date with family events (often during key years for world history—one is set during the Kennedy assassination, one during the moon walk). The child actors who starred in the first pilot film continued in their roles as they grew up, and the stories of their families were woven into the happy saga of poor but honest folk. The only actor to be replaced was Richard Thompson, who played John (John-Boy), Jr. for the first five seasons, then left to pursue his movie career – anyone remember his Mark Hamill-wannabe turn in *Battle Beyond the Stars*? As a result, John-Boy was packed off to college, returning for the last two series in the guise of Robert Wightman.

By the end of the show's lifetime, four of the children had moved out, and the boys were in the services as it was World War II. Mary Ellen, the eldest daughter (Jody Norton-Taylor) has also married an idealistic doctor who was reported killed at Pearl Harbor. Toward the end of the run, the plots got a little convoluted, and Mary Ellen's husband was revealed to be living incommunicado in a nearby city, because he'd become impotent from his war injuries. Meanwhile, fiery redhead Jason, the second-eldest brother, was working as a pianist in the local honky-tonk bar, and the baby of the family, Elizabeth (Kami Cotler), had exhibited her fears of growing up by producing poltergeist activity when she hit puberty.

Many of the younger actors went on to indifferent careers as bit players in TV movies. Richard Thomas was by far the most successful, with over 55 movies under his belt, including roles in Stephen King's *It* and the title role in Hank Williams, Jr.'s biopic. By contrast Eric Scott, who played the slightly less ginger-haired middle brother, Ben, was the least. He made just five appearances after the show ended. Nowadays he's vice-president of Century Express, the Los Angeles-based courier firm he co-founded.

There are two reasons to kill people on television: to boost Kleenex sales, and to shock viewers. You expect emotional manipulation from sentimental family dramas, but in the end few TV shows can resist tugging at your heart strings . . .

## SHOCK JOCKS

**The Shield** You think Terry Crowley is going to be a major player—he's in the main credits and everything, and part of the SWAT team around whom the series is built. Then team leader Vic learns he's a plant (the team aren't exactly boy scouts), and guns him down during a raid.

**The Sopranos** Tony Soprano gets through a lot of body bags, but reaches a peak of brutality when he beats Ralphie Cifaretto to death because he thinks Ralphie is trying to scam him, then carries his head around in a bowling bag before burying it.

**ER** Dr. Romano, having had his arm sliced off by a helicopter blade during a moment of carelessness in one season of *ER*, is just getting the hang of being a one-handed surgeon when he's crushed to death by another helicopter which falls out of the sky onto him. To add insult to injury, the homophobic doc is commemorated by a gay and lesbian endowment.

**24** Agent Jack Bauer's wife Teri is rescued after a day from hell, involving her being raped and tortured, Jack has thwarted the terrorists, and you're ready for the relaxing ending . . . when suddenly Teri's kidnapped again, and this time her throat is cut.

**Lost** The opening sequence features an unfortunate soul who wanders too close to the crashed plane's still whirling turbine and is sucked in.

## TEARJERKERS

**M*A*S*H** Colonel Blake finally gets to go home, but his plane is shot down and there are no survivors.

**NYPD Blue** Unexpectedly, heartthrob Bobby Simone develops a heart complaint and slowly dies—you expect a reprieve, but nothing comes.

**Ally McBeal** Ally's true and lost love, Billy, becomes a male chauvinist pig and "bleaches his head," but it's only because he has a brain tumor and is about to drop dead in the courtroom.

**Buffy the Vampire Slayer** Joss Whedon killed off the title character twice (as the finale to seasons 1 and 5), but the sudden death of Buffy's mum, Joyce, from a brain tumor provides the show's most harrowing plot line.

# "FLIPPER LIVES IN A WORLD FULL OF WONDER . . ."

Flipper the Dolphin's aquatic adventures began in two successful feature films—*Flipper* (1963) and *Flipper's New Adventure* (1964)—which were largely the brainchild of Ricou Browning. By 1964, a TV series had been created; Browning wrote and directed many episodes. He was a highly qualified diver and had experienced his first taste of Hollywood glamor when he was called upon to shamble about in a rubber suit in *The Creature from the Black Lagoon* (1957) and its various sequels, including *Revenge of the Creature*, and *The Creature Walks Among Us*.

Browning later set himself up as an underwater filming specialist and worked on several Bond films. He recruited his Atlantic bottlenose dolphin star from Milton Santini, who had trained a dolphin called Mitzi to allow his son to ride on her back and play ball. Mitzi starred in the original film, and Santini went on to open Flipper's Sea School in the Florida Keys. Mitzi died at Grassy Key, Florida, on June 25, 1971, at age 22. She was replaced by several dolphins from the Miami Seaquarium, which took to proclaiming itself "The Home of Flipper." Bebe, the last dolphin to appear in the role, was 40 when she died in 1997.

> **They had two Partridge families at the end of all the callbacks and we shot two shows. Shirley was the Mom in each. David [Cassidy], Susan [Dey], and the other kids were all in one family, and I was in the other family with a bunch of other kids. The other family got the job. But Jerry [Paris] went to an editing booth and edited me into a scene with Reuben that I was never in. So I'm talking back and forth with Dave Madden and it never really happened. It was Hollywood magic. He showed the producers, they hired me on the spot, and we shot a third show and I got the job.**
>
> Danny Bonaduce (Danny Partridge) on how he nearly didn't make it into one of the most successful family shows of the 1970s

# Grab bag

EVERYTHING THAT DIDN'T FIT BUT WAS TOO
GOOD TO LEAVE OUT

The Super Bowl takes four out of ten spots in the US Top 10, and by the time you add in the Olympics, sport accounts for half of the most popular shows stateside, unlike the UK, where soaps rule the roost. For ordinary cult TV shows to compete they need to be something special indeed!

77% of people watching TV on February 28, 1983 were tuned in to watch the final episode of *M*A*S*H*.

76% of people watching TV on November 21, 1980 wanted to see who shot J. R. on *Dallas.*

73% of viewers were watching *Super Bowl XVI* (The San Francisco 49ers vs. the Cincinnati Bengals) on January 24, 1982.

71% of Americans watching TV were viewing the final episode of *Roots* on January 30, 1977.

70% watched *Super Bowl XX* (The Chicago Bears vs. the New England Patriots) on January 25, 1986.

69% tuned in to *Super Bowl XVII* to see if the Washington Redskins would beat the Miami Dolphins on January 30, 1983.

67% of viewers were watching *Super Bowl XII*, when the Dallas Cowboys played the Denver Broncos, on January 15, 1978.

65% of people watching TV wanted to enjoy the spectacle of *Gone with the Wind* (Part 1) on November 7, 1976.

64%, just 1% fewer, returned the next night for the second half.

64% were drawn by the all-US **Tonya Harding–Nancy Kerrigan skate-off** at the 17th Winter Olympics, on February 23, 1994.

> **Today, watching television often means fighting, violence, and foul language—and that's just deciding who gets to hold the remote control.**
>
> American humorist Donna Gephart

*The Benny Hill Show* was sold to more than 140 countries around the world, and although regarded as sexist and outdated in Britain by the 1980s, Jacques Tati, Maurice Chevalier, Greta Garbo, and Chaplin were all fans of Hill's slapstick humor.

When Benny Hill died in 1992, at age 68, his body lay undiscovered for days. He left a £10 million fortune, yet never owned a house or a car, preferring to rent a modest flat within walking distance of the Teddington Studios where he taped his show.

When he died he was living in a small house in the suburbs, subsisting on cheap tinned food, while his drawers were stuffed with uncashed checks. He was known as a bit of an obsessive when it came to work, and had few close friends.

After his death, rumors about his sex life began to surface, including allegations that he was rather too close to his mother. Hill had never married, but he did propose twice, and on both occasions was rejected. Friends say one of the women was Annette Andre, then a star of *Randall & Hopkirk Deceased*, an unusual comedy detective show in which one of the title duo was a ghost, and that after being turned down he left the room whenever the show came on TV.

According to Bob Monkhouse, Hill once told him he had a fantasy about being pleasured orally by factory girls who would call him "Mr. Hill," and be "respectful" to him. He had relationships with several "Hill's Angels," the eye candy from his show. Hill's head Angel, in every sense of the word, was Sue Upton, who joined the show at the age of 20 and claimed: "In all the years I've known Benny, I've never heard him swear, raise his voice, lose his temper or say anything disrespectful to a girl." Another later reported: "I always kept my knickers on and he would never touch me. Once when he did try to touch me up, he did it wearing rubber gloves."

*They Saved Hitler's Brain! (And Transplanted it into a Shark)*

*The Girl Whose Head Fell Off*

*Dough Boys—Danger on the Pizza Delivery Route*

*Seal Slaughter*

*The Nazi Cookbook: Recipes from the Third Reich*

*American Bicycle*

*When the Shark (with Hitler's Brain) Attacks!*

*Crime Scene Photo Album*

*Midnight Autopsy*

## THE STRANGEST NAME FOR A TV SHOW – EVER!

The right name is the first line of attack when trying to entice the viewing public to tune in to your show. You can go for enigmatic and brief (*Lost*). You can choose dynamic words (*When Games Attack*, sadly not about people getting their fingers torn off playing Hungry Hippos or losing an eye to Buckaroo). You can suggest the unlikely (*The Boy Whose Skin Fell Off*). Or you can just make no sense at all.

*Ball Trap on the Cote Sauvage* (1989) was a BBC Screen One drama written by Andrew Davies, which savagely scrutinizes the relationships of a bunch of British tourists at a French campsite. We see everything through the eyes of the Marriots, played by Jack Shepherd and Zoe Wanamaker, whose cosy commentary on the antics of their fellow holidaymakers is disrupted by the arrival of Early Bird, a free-spirited woman married to a boorish husband. The play upholds the Screen One tradition of disturbing sexual content, nihilism, and subversiveness.

### 1957 – Piss

"I wouldn't piss on him if he went up in flames. I'm an Elvis man meself." – Teddy Boy, when asked his opinion of Bill Haley live on a *BBC News* bulletin.

### 1965 – F**k

Kenneth Tynan, on the late-night satirical show *BBC3*. One Tory MP insists that Tynan should be hung for the offense.

### 1967 – Too Bloody Much

"This is the end of civilization as we know it" thunders Mary Whitehouse, having seen an episode of *Till Death Do Us Part*, in which she counted 44 uses of "bloody."

### 1968 – C**t

Magazine publisher Felix Dennis becomes the first man to use the c-word on British television, during a debate on the counterculture, in *The Frost Report*.

### 1974 – Naff off

To avoid offending, the writers of *Porridge* introduce the term "Naff" (from the Australian expression "Nasty as f**k").

### 1976 – Rotters

Steve Jones of The Sex Pistols appears live on *The Reg Grundy Show*, and calls the host a "f***ing rotter" after he suggests meeting Siouxsie Sioux after the broadcast for some unspecified hanky panky. Grundy is strongly censured, then fined, for antagonising the band on live TV, asking them to swear more. The Pistols later successfully defend the use of "Bollocks'" in their album title "Never Mind The Bollocks" as an innofensive Anglo-Saxon term.

### 1993 – Poodle Fanciers

"Thank you very much, you motherf*****s!" Pete Sampras tells the Wimbledon crowd.

### 2003 – Extreme F**king

Gordon Ramsey's *Hell's Kitchen UK* – 43 uses of the f-word in one episode. Ramsey is probably known by more people for his swearing than his cooking, but the authors can attest to the fact that he's a f**king good cook, too.

### 2004 – Cocksucker

The HBO Western *Deadwood* has become notorious for using the word "cocksucker" about once a minute per episode. Keith Caradine clocks up an even more impressive 22 c**ts in two minutes playing Wild Bill Hickok.

1. *Jerry Springer, The Opera* (2004)
immense amounts of swearing, Christ in a diaper, etc.
(63,000 complaints, 55,000 of them before it had even started)

2. *The Last Temptation of Christ* (2001)
Christ doesn't die on the cross and raises a family (1,554)

3. *Brass Eye* (2001)
Pedophile Special – which many people failed to realise was a parody (992)

4. *Spitting Image* (1992)
Puppet images of God (341)

5. *Living With Michael Jackson* (2003)
Martin Bashir proves as nauseating as his subject matter (171)

6. *The Bill* (2002)
Two policemen kiss on popular mid-evening cop show (170)

7. *Queer As Folk* (1999)
Underage gay sex (163)

8. *Against Nature* (1997)
Documentary compares environmentalists to Nazis (151)

9. *Without Walls: Hell's Angel* (1994)
Painted less than complimentary portrait of Mother Teresa (134)

10. *Undercover Britain* (1998)
Unfairness in documentary about security at gun clubs (123)

*Source: ITC*

---

**You're beginning to think that the tube is reality and that your own lives are unreal . . . In God's name, you people are the real thing; we're the illusion.**

Howard Beale (Peter Finch) in Paddy Chayevski's film *Network*

---

# MISSING IN ACTION

**10 characters who were frequently mentioned
on TV shows but never seen:**

Captain Mainwaring's wife Elizabeth (*Dad's Army*)

Niles Crane's wife Maris (*Frasier*)

Karen's wealthy husband Stanley (*Will & Grace*)

"Er indoors," Arthur Daley's missus (*Minder*)

Len Mangel, Mrs. Mangel's husband (*Neighbours*)

Our Vera, Lily Savage's prostitute sister (*The Lily Savage Show*)

Norm Peterson's wife Vera (*Cheers*)

Beverley Macca, Denise's rival (*The Royle Family*)

Hyacinth Bucket's son Sheridan (*Keeping Up Appearances*)

Ben from the Postroom (*The Smoking Room*)

## THE YEAR OF THE SEX OLYMPICS

Back in 1968, the playwright Nigel Kneale predicted the rise of reality TV in his prescient BBC Television play, *The Year of the Sex Olympics*. Kneale had famously adapted Orwell's *Nineteen Eighty-Four* for the Beeb 14 years earlier, and concerns about media control were still obviously uppermost in his mind.

*The Year of the Sex Olympics* presents a future society divided into "low-drives" and "hi-drives," where the latter have all the important jobs and control the former by feeding them a constant diet of TV pornography. The accidental death of a protester during the Sex Olympics gets a huge audience response, which causes the TV Controller (played by Leonard Rossiter) to think of a new kind of TV show, on starring ordinary people. He creates *The Live Life Show*, featuring a family stranded on a remote Scottish island (shades of *Castaway* 2000). When ratings start to decline the producers introduce a psychopath who begins stalking the family, which makes it compelling viewing once again.

Cuddly Noel Edmonds' BBC vehicle *The Late Late Breakfast show*, was hurriedly taken off the air in 1986 after one of the show's trademark stunts went horribly wrong: 25-year-old Michael Lush was taking part in the "Whirly Wheel" segment of the show, where a member of the public is selected to do a stunt. He was supposed to fall out of a box on a bungee cord, but due to poor safety checks by an improperly qualified supervisor he fell to his death. However, after two years cooling his heels Edmonds was back on Saturday prime-time with *Noel's Saturday Roadshow*, and went on to inflict the likes of Mr. Blobby on the ever-forgiving nation.

The most common victims of TV shows kill themselves. In 1997, the first Swedish version of *Survivor* (then known as *Expedition: Robinson*) became notorious when Sinisa Savija, the first contestant to be voted off the island, committed suicide, reportedly unable to face the public rejection. Najai "Nitro" Turpin, one of the boxers who appeared on *The Contender*, reportedly shot himself in his car on Valentine's Day, 2004, at the age of just 23, before the show was aired, as did Carina Stephenson, a 17-year-old from Yorkshire, England, after she'd finished filming *The Colony*, a History Channel show recreating the lives of convicts sent to Australia.

You should also beware when a member of your family gets involved in reality TV. When Deleese Williams was selected as a potential contestant for the popular US transformation show *Extreme Makeover*, a TV crew flew to her Texas home and filmed her family, including sister Kellie, talking about her appearance. Then Deleese was deselected because her treatments wouldn't heal quickly enough for the shooting schedule. Subsequently, Kellie killed herself, and Deleese is suing the program's creators for $1 million, claiming it was anguish over the cruel things she said about her sister that caused Kellie to take her own life.

> **Good heavens, television is something you appear on, you don't watch.**
>
> Noël Coward

Sometimes you get the sense that talk show bookers want the guests to misbehave. But others get an unpleasant surprise when their crowd-pleasers turn into monsters:

1.  Oliver Reed (drunk on *The Word*, drunk on *After Dark*, drunk on *Saturday Night at the Mill*, drunk on *Aspel* – barking, growling, boggling his eyes, ripping his shirt open, and almost certainly soiling himself, not to mention indulging in pub singer antics)

2.  Tara Palmer-Tompkinson (coked out of her mind on *The Frank Skinner Show*)

3.  Meg Ryan (pissed off on *Parkinson* – "If I were you, I'd wind it up")

4.  George Best (drunk on *Wogan* – "Terry, I like screwing")

5.  Anne Bancroft (monosyllabic on *Wogan*; even his cheeky chappie's charm failed to elicit more than a curt "yes" or "no")

6.  Lynne Perrie (with a face so swollen from plastic surgery she could hardly speak on *The Word*)

7.  Tracey Emin (fabulously stroppy due to drink / painkillers combo on a *Newsnight* Turner Prize special)

8.  Shane MacGowan (drunk and incomprehensible gurgler on *Frank Skinner*)

9.  Grace Jones (battering Russell Harty for not giving her enough attention)

10. David Blaine (staring spookily and making hand gestures to protect himself from evil – or perhaps bemused host Eamon Holmes – on the GMTV breakfast show)

> **For God's sake go down to reception and get rid of the lunatic who's down there. He says he's got a machine for seeing by wireless!**
>
> Editor of the *Daily Express* on being told that television inventor John Logie Baird was in reception

> **Television is the first truly democratic culture, the first culture available to everybody and entirely governed by what the people want. The most terrifying thing is what people do want.**
>
> Clive Barnes (who was spookily prescient, since reality TV hadn't yet bombarded the networks when he wrote this)

## BIG BROTHER RULES THE WORLD

The most successful reality TV show in the world is, without a doubt, *Big Brother*, which began in 2000 in a comparatively modest way on Dutch TV. Now Africa, Australia, Bahrain, Belgium, Brazil, Bulgaria, Chile, Denmark, Ecuador, Germany, Greece, Italy, Mexico, the Netherlands, Poland, Romania, Spain, South Africa, Sweden, the UK and the US have all produced their own versions. It's a competitive market: According to Nielson Media Research more than half the programs on American TV are now reality shows, and worldwide they account for nearly 70% of programming.

Modest fame, erratic fortune, and as many column inches in *Heat* as they like await the UK participants when they get out of "The House", provided they're willing to bare their souls, claim to have shagged someone under the duvet, have makeovers, gain and lose weight spectacularly and attend every launch party going.

But not all *Big Brother* contestants get what they want out of the show. In 2001, the final seven contestants in the Danish version all walked out together, bringing the show to a screeching halt. In France police had to use tear gas to break up crowds of activists keen to use the show to get their point across, and in Bahrain more than a thousand protesters threatened to storm their version of the *Big Brother* house for undermining Islamic values, causing recording to stop. Watching the UK show would really have gotten their goat—featuring, as it did, a gay winner in 2001, and a transsexual in 2004.

**Art may imitate life,
but life imitates TV.**

Ani Difranco

# FURTHER READING

*Loony Tunes & Merrie Melodies*, Jerry Beck, Will Friedwald
*The Complete Directory to Prime Time Network and Cable TV Shows (1946–present)*, Tim Brooks & Earle Marsh
*The Ultimate TV Guide*, Jon E. Lewis and Penny Stempel
*Clint Eastwood*, Daniel OBrien
*The Oxford History of the American West,*
Ed Clyde A. Milner II, Carol A. O'Connor, Martha A. Sandweiss
*Encyclopedia of TV Science Fiction*, Roger Fulton
*The Guinness Book of Sitcoms*, Rod Taylor
*The Encyclopedia Shatnerica*, Robert E. Schnakenberg
*Halliwell's Television Companion*, Leslie Halliwell with Philip Purser
*Fawlty Towers*, Morris Bright & Robert Ross
*Who's Who on Television*, Eddie Pedder
*This Is Their Life*, Jonathan Meades
*Glued to the Box*, Clive James
*Soap Box*, Hilary Kingsley
*Television's Greatest Hits*, Paul Gambaccini & Rod Taylor
*TV Babylon*, Paul Donnelley
*Beam Me Up, Scotty*, James Doohan with Peter David
*Journal of Criminal Justice & Popular Culture Vol XII 2005*, New York Times

*http://tv50.org.uk*
*www.bbc.co.uk/cult*
*www.sitcomsonline.com*
*www.78rpm.co.uk*
*www.magicdragon.com/UltimateSF*
*www.twinpeaks.org*
*www.snopes.com*
*www.retroweb.com*
*www.legendsofamerica.com*
*www.museum.tv*
*www.davidlynch.com*

# INDEX

# INDEX

**Gods of Rock**

By Rob Fitzpatrick and Mark Roland

**Kings of Comedy**

By Johnny Acton and Paul Webb

**Movie Idols**

By John Wrathall and Mick Molloy